Ryo Tatsuki Prophesies for 2025 and Beyond

Andrew Parry

Published by Andrew Parry, 2025.

RYO TATSUKI PROPHESIES FOR 2025 AND BEYOND

First edition. April 21, 2025.

Copyright © 2025 Andrew Parry.

ISBN: 979-8230639008

Written by Andrew Parry.

Table of Contents

Introduction: The Dreamer Who Drew Tomorrow 1

Origins of a Visionary 3

The First Prophetic Dream 4

Sketching the Future 6

The Making of The Future I Saw 8

Dreams That Shook the World 10

Kobe Earthquake Foretold 12

Princess Diana: A Premonition 14

Freddie Mercury's Final Note 16

The 2011 Tsunami: A Predicted Tragedy 18

The Virus of 2020: Foreseen 20

The Unpublished Dreams 22

The Complete Version: Revisiting the Past 24

The Symbolism in Her Art 26

The Left Eye: Window to the Past 28

The Right Eye: Glimpse into Tomorrow 30

The Old Man in Dreams 32

The Cracked Earth Vision 34

The Boiling Sea: A Metaphor? 36

The Mt. Fuji Eruption That Wasn't 38

The 15-Year Pattern 40

Interpreting the Unfulfilled 42

The July 2025 Catastrophe 44

The 4:18 AM Alarm 46

The Undersea Volcano between Japan and the Philippines 48

The Mega-Tsunami Warning 50

The Impact on Japan's Coastline 52

Taiwan and Indonesia: In the Path 54

The Northern Mariana Islands Threatened 56

The Date with Destiny: July 5, 2025 58

The Aftermath: Predictions Beyond 2025 60

The Yokohama Tsunami Vision 62

The 2026 Summer Floods 64

The Role of Dreams in Prophecy 66

Science Meets the Supernatural 68

Sceptics and Believers 70

The Media's Role in Spreading the Word 72

The Cult Following of Her Manga 74

The Auction Frenzy: Collecting Prophecies 76

The Ethics of Predicting Disasters 78

Preparing for the Foreseen 80

The Psychological Impact of Prophecies 82

The Global Response to Her Warnings 84

The Intersection of Art and Clairvoyance 86

The Legacy of Ryo Tatsuki 88

Lessons from the Past Predictions 90

The Cultural Significance in Japan 92

The Influence on Modern Manga Artists 94

The Spiritual Interpretations 96

The Role of Intuition in Creativity 98

The Debate: Coincidence or Clairvoyance? 100

The Future of Prophetic Art 102

The Responsibility of the Prophet 104

The Personal Toll of Seeing the Future 106

The Line between Dream and Reality 108

The Evolution of Her Predictions 110

The Global Implications of Her Visions 112

The Continuation of Her Work... 114

The Public's Role in Heeding Warnings.. 116

The Final Chapter: Awaiting July 2025 118

Introduction: The Dreamer Who Drew Tomorrow

In the quiet city of Tokyo, far from the noise of press conferences and headlines, lived a woman with a sketchbook and a peculiar relationship to time. Her name was **Ryo Tatsuki** — a manga artist, illustrator, and dreamer whose life was as quiet as her prophecies were unsettling. She wasn't famous in her early years. She didn't seek attention. She worked in solitude, recorded her dreams with a calm precision, and quietly published a series of self-made books — most notably *The Future I Saw* — that would later be seen not as speculative fiction, but as *something else entirely*.

Ryo was born in Japan and lived most of her life in or near Tokyo, a city that pulses with modernity but holds deep undercurrents of spirituality and stillness. From a young age, she experienced vivid dreams — not the typical swirling chaos of sleep, but scenes, places, and moments that felt *too specific, too structured, too real* to be random. These weren't dreams you forget over breakfast. These were dreams that woke her up at exact times. Dreams with imagery she couldn't shake. So she did what artists do — she drew them.

What set Ryo apart wasn't just the content of her visions, but *how* she recorded them. She didn't embellish. She didn't interpret. She simply sketched what she saw, often with accompanying dates, times, and brief captions — rarely more than a sentence or two. Some of these images were subtle. A clock stuck at 4:18 AM. A masked crowd walking silently through a city. A coastal skyline drowned in still water. At the time of publication, they felt like emotional metaphors. But years later, as real-world events began to unfold — the 1995 Kobe earthquake, the 2011 tsunami, the global pandemic of 2020 — readers began returning to her early pages and asking the same question:

How did she see this coming?

This book is not just a biography of Ryo Tatsuki, though her life and process are examined here in careful detail. Nor is it merely a catalog of her dreams — though many of her most haunting predictions are explored, from the already fulfilled to those that still linger on the horizon. This is a book about *meaning, memory*, and the quiet possibility that some people see beyond the veil of now. It is a reflection on intuition, on art, and on the strange places where dreams and disasters intersect.

The early chapters explore Ryo's childhood, her emergence as an artist, and the first time she recorded a dream that later aligned with a global event. We dive into her style — her choice of medium, her use of negative space, and the recurring symbols that populate her visions. We examine her most widely discussed predictions: the 2011 tsunami, the death of Princess Diana, the COVID-19 pandemic, and her unsettling vision of July 5, 2025.

From there, we move into interpretation — the symbolism in her work, the recurring motifs (water, silence, time), and the emotional texture that threads through every page. We discuss how her work was received around the world — by believers and skeptics alike — and how her drawings became a kind of underground scripture for those who felt the world growing stranger by the day.

Later chapters delve into the psychology of prophecy, the role of dreams in human culture, and the debate over whether her drawings are clairvoyant or coincidental. We look at the communities her work has inspired — from artists to scientists to spiritual seekers — and how her influence is shaping the next generation of dream-oriented creatives.

The final chapters turn toward the future. What happens when a date she recorded — so specific, so mysterious — finally arrives? What will July 5, 2025, mean to the world, regardless of what unfolds that morning? And more importantly, what has her work already *taught us* about presence, preparedness, and perception?

This is not a book about fear. It is a book about *attention*. Ryo Tatsuki never shouted her message. She whispered it in pencil, on paper, in silence. Her dreams were not doomsday declarations. They were invitations — to look more closely, to feel more deeply, and to remember that the future may already be speaking... softly, patiently... in the places we least expect it.

This book is for anyone who has ever woken from a dream and thought, *That felt too real.*

It's for those who have sensed something coming without knowing what.

And it's for those who wonder — as Ryo did — what we might see if we learned how to *listen in our sleep*.

Origins of a Visionary

In the vibrant tapestry of Japan's manga industry, few figures stand out as uniquely as Ryo Tatsuki. Emerging in the 1970s, Tatsuki carved a niche for herself not just through her artistic prowess but also through an uncanny ability that blurred the lines between creativity and clairvoyance.

Born in Japan, Tatsuki's early life was steeped in the rich cultural milieu that would later influence her work. By the mid-1970s, she had embarked on her journey as a manga artist, debuting in 1975 and quickly gaining recognition for her distinctive style and storytelling. However, it wasn't merely her artistic talent that set her apart; it was the vivid, often unsettling dreams that began to permeate her consciousness.

Starting in the late 1960s, Tatsuki experienced dreams that were strikingly detailed and, as time would reveal, eerily prophetic. These were not fleeting images but vivid narratives that compelled her to document them meticulously. By 1980, she had begun recording these dreams in a personal journal, capturing visions that ranged from natural disasters to significant global events. This practice became a cornerstone of her creative process, intertwining her subconscious experiences with her artistic endeavors.

In 1999, Tatsuki published "The Future I Saw" (*Watashi ga Mita Mirai*), a manga that compiled 15 of her most compelling dreams from 1985 to 1999. At the time of its release, the work garnered modest attention, appreciated for its unique blend of personal narrative and speculative foresight. However, it wasn't until years later that the true impact of her work would be realized.

One of the most striking aspects of Tatsuki's dreams was their specificity. She documented visions that included the death of Freddie Mercury in 1991, the devastating Kobe earthquake in 1995, and the tragic passing of Princess Diana in 1997. Perhaps most notably, she foresaw the Great East Japan Earthquake of 2011, a catastrophic event that claimed thousands of lives and left an indelible mark on the nation's collective memory. In her manga, a particular dream dated March 11, 2011, eerily coincided with the actual date of the disaster, leading many to revisit her work with renewed interest and a sense of awe.

The resurgence of attention to Tatsuki's work was not limited to retrospective validation. In the years following the 2011 earthquake, readers and scholars alike delved into her manga, uncovering a series of predictions that had seemingly come to fruition. This led to a re-evaluation of her work, transforming it from a niche artistic endeavor into a subject of widespread intrigue and discussion.

Tatsuki's journey from a manga artist to a figure of prophetic fascination underscores the profound connection between art and the subconscious. Her experiences challenge conventional understandings of creativity, suggesting that the boundaries between imagination and premonition may be more porous than previously thought. As we explore her life and work, we are invited to consider the possibilities that lie at the intersection of dreams, art, and the enigmatic currents of time.

In the chapters that follow, we will delve deeper into the specific dreams that have captivated audiences, the cultural and scientific responses to her predictions, and the ongoing discourse surrounding the nature of foresight and its place in our understanding of the world. Through the lens of Ryo Tatsuki's extraordinary journey, we embark on an exploration of the mysterious and often uncharted territories of human consciousness.

The First Prophetic Dream

Ryo Tatsuki was still a teenager when it happened. She had just begun to take her drawing seriously, mostly scribbling in the margins of her schoolbooks and copying her favorite manga characters in quiet corners of her bedroom. She wasn't yet a manga artist. She wasn't yet someone people paid attention to. She was just a quiet girl in Tokyo with a head full of stories and a subtle sense that her dreams meant something. Not in the dramatic sense — not yet — but in that strange, unsettled way where your dream clings to you for days, as if it were trying to tell you something and wouldn't let go.

The first prophetic dream came in the summer of 1982. It was a humid, restless night. The cicadas outside screamed into the darkness and the little electric fan on her desk turned back and forth in mechanical rhythm. She drifted to sleep thinking of an idea she'd had for a manga panel — a romantic scene on a bridge, typical for her imagination at the time. But what she experienced instead had nothing to do with romance. It was chaos. And it was terrifyingly vivid.

In the dream, Ryo stood on a street she didn't recognize — maybe Tokyo, maybe not — the buildings were cracked open like broken teeth and people were screaming, running. She could feel the ground beneath her shaking, like a slow and angry heartbeat, rising from somewhere deep underground. Power lines danced above her, windows shattered in waves, and the sea was far too close, as if the coastline had swallowed up half the city. She saw a calendar in the debris with the number "1995" circled. No month, no day. Just the year.

When she woke up, her bedsheets were soaked in sweat, her heart pounding like she'd run a marathon. At first, she did what most people would do — she dismissed it. A nightmare. Probably something she saw on the news. Maybe the result of watching too many intense anime late at night. But something about it haunted her. It wasn't just a dream. It felt like it had *happened*. Like she'd *been* there. As if it hadn't come from her imagination at all — but from someplace else entirely.

That morning, Ryo did something she'd never done before. She took her school sketchbook and, instead of her usual manga doodles, began drawing what she saw in the dream. The cracked street. The people running. The tilted skyline. She sketched the trembling electricity poles and the sea that didn't belong there. In the corner of the drawing, she wrote in pencil: "Dream. 1995."

She didn't tell anyone. Not yet. It felt too strange, and honestly, who would care? People dream about disasters all the time. But still, she kept that sketchbook and continued to record the more powerful dreams she had, especially the ones that gave her that same deep, electric feeling in her chest. Something real. Something more than a dream.

Over the next few years, the dreams began to come more often. Most of them were fragmented and hard to understand, but a few had that same intensity — that sense of being in the middle of something that hadn't happened yet. She saw people she didn't recognize. Places that didn't yet exist. Dates. Emotions. Headlines. Sometimes they were flashes. Other times they were full scenes, like watching a movie in slow motion, unable to move or change anything, only observe.

And then, in January of 1995, it happened.

The Great Hanshin Earthquake struck Kobe with a force that shattered the city. Over 6,000 people died. Ryo watched the news coverage in horror. Buildings had fallen exactly like in her drawing. Streets split open. Power lines swinging. The nightmare had walked out of her subconscious and into the real world. Her sketch from over a decade earlier looked like a premonition.

For the first time, she wondered if her mind was somehow tapping into something unseen — a current that ran beneath time. Her pencil, it seemed, had captured the future.

That was the moment she stopped being just a manga artist in training. That was the moment she started documenting her dreams with purpose. With urgency. She bought a new notebook and called it what it truly was — a dream journal. In it, she began writing down everything with timestamps, with sketches, with every detail she could remember. And she noticed something else too — the prophetic dreams had a different texture than ordinary ones. They were quieter. Slower. Heavy with atmosphere. And always, always left her physically shaken when she woke up.

She never once thought of herself as a prophet. She wasn't a psychic. She didn't predict things on demand. She wasn't trying to impress anyone. Her only goal was to *record*. And maybe, in some small way, *warn*. Because what good is seeing the future if you can't do something about it?

But the world wouldn't know about that first dream — not until 1999, when she published *The Future I Saw*, a self-contained manga that compiled 15 of her most powerful prophetic dreams. The 1995 earthquake made it into the book, of course. And it gave her work credibility. People started paying attention. At first, it was manga fans. Then journalists. Then scientists. And eventually, believers and skeptics from all corners of society.

But none of them had seen her that night in 1982, sitting in the heat with a sketchpad on her lap, drawing out a disaster no one had lived through yet. No one saw how quiet it was. How personal. How terrifying. How lonely.

That first prophetic dream was the beginning of something she didn't ask for — a path that would make her both respected and feared. And that's what sets Ryo Tatsuki apart from so many others who've claimed to see the future. She never sought fame or recognition. She only wanted to understand what her dreams were showing her, and why.

And that question — why her? — would follow her for the rest of her life.

Sketching the Future

Ryo Tatsuki never considered herself special. She wasn't the type to chase the spotlight, and she certainly didn't expect that her dreams would one day spark global fascination. She simply saw the world in a different way — through images, emotions, and flashes of the unknown. For her, the future didn't come in a blinding vision or an angelic voice from the clouds. It came in dreams. And from the moment she woke up, her instinct was always the same: draw it.

Sketching, for Ryo, was more than a creative outlet. It was her language. When words failed to describe the eerie clarity of what she'd seen in the night, her pencil filled in the blanks. The lines, the shading, the perspective — they all carried more than artistic intention. They carried warning. Revelation. A strange kind of responsibility. Over time, her drawings became records. Not of what was, but of what *might* be.

She didn't sketch casually. She did it with intensity, often sitting for hours after a dream to capture every possible detail before it faded. Some dreams were visual in a cinematic sense — long sequences, vivid colors, coherent narratives. Others were surreal, nonlinear, disjointed images that made no immediate sense. But even in those moments, she trusted her hands to draw what her conscious mind couldn't fully process. The future, as it came to her, didn't always arrive with instructions. It arrived with symbols.

One dream left her with an image of a broken bridge hanging over a river, the water surging underneath. People stood frozen on either side, unable to cross. She didn't know what it meant at the time, but she drew it anyway. Years later, she would revisit that sketch and realize it bore a disturbing resemblance to a collapsed bridge in China following a sudden flood. The dream had no date attached to it — just an emotional weight, a visual truth. She didn't predict the event. She *captured* it, as if her mind had taken a snapshot from time's filing cabinet and handed it back to her with no explanation.

That's what made her work so haunting. The sketches were not interpreted *after* the fact to fit events. They were dated, drawn, and forgotten — until the real-world tragedy mirrored what was already on the page. These moments built slowly over the years, forming a pattern too strange to ignore. Even the skeptics had to pause when they saw the timestamps. How do you explain drawing the death of a famous singer — years before it happened — in a quiet corner of a sketchbook?

Ryo never drew for attention. Her manga wasn't marketed as prophecy. It was, to her, a journal in visual form. A means of mapping a world she didn't entirely understand. She wasn't trying to build a cult of belief. She wasn't asking anyone to change their lives or prepare for doomsday. She was just doing what she had always done — drawing the truth as she saw it, even if that truth hadn't happened yet.

The process of sketching after a dream became something like ritual. She would wake, heart racing, and immediately reach for her notebook. Sometimes the image was so powerful that she didn't even need to think — it was like her hands were remembering more than her conscious brain. There was no time for polish or perfection. It was urgent. Almost sacred. Get it down before it slips away.

Her workspace was modest — a desk in a small room, shelves lined with manga volumes and old drawing supplies. It looked like the studio of any ordinary artist, but to her, it was a gateway. The pencil became her key. The page, her portal. And the act of drawing? That was the moment the dream became real, transformed into something she could point to and say, "I saw this."

There's something deeply human in the way she chose to process the future. Not with declarations, not with television appearances or dramatic predictions, but with images. Private, intimate, urgent sketches that came from the deepest recesses of her sleep. She could have chosen to forget them. Most people would have. But something compelled her to keep going. And with each new drawing, her archive of possible futures grew.

Years later, when she compiled *The Future I Saw*, readers were stunned to learn how many of the drawings matched real-world events — sometimes down to uncanny details. The Kobe earthquake. The death of Princess Diana. The 2011 tsunami. These weren't artistic impressions after the fact. They were sketches that existed long before the events they mirrored.

But there's another side to this — the sketches that *haven't* come true. The ones still waiting in the quiet pages of her notebooks, holding mysteries we haven't yet unraveled. Among them is her now-famous vision of a massive disaster she saw taking place in July 2025 — a dream that haunts many and remains hotly debated. In that drawing, water surges across city streets, and an old man appears in the background, expression unreadable. She didn't know what it meant, only that she had seen it. And she drew it.

Ryo never claimed to understand the source of her visions. Whether they were fragments of collective consciousness, echoes from other timelines, or just extraordinary coincidences, she never tried to explain them. She only tried to capture them honestly. Drawing was her way of coping — and perhaps her way of warning, in the only way she knew how.

She wasn't trying to be a prophet. She was an artist with a pencil, caught between the boundaries of dream and destiny.

And every time she picked up that pencil, she wasn't just drawing — she was *sketching the future*.

The Making of The Future I Saw

By the late 1990s, Ryo Tatsuki had already been drawing her dreams for nearly two decades. They filled notebooks, loose sheets, tucked folders, and the backs of receipts. Some were simple pencil sketches — raw, immediate, barely legible — while others had taken form as full, detailed illustrations of scenes so vivid they could have come straight from a film. But none of it was ever intended to be published. Her dream journals were private. Intimate. Sacred. They weren't drawn to impress; they were drawn to document. That was until someone close to her — a friend or perhaps an editor — asked a simple question: *What if you turned these into a manga?*

At first, Ryo didn't take the idea seriously. She had always separated her professional manga work from her dream sketches. One was for public consumption; the other was too strange, too personal. But the more she thought about it, the more she realized that she wasn't the only one who might benefit from seeing what she'd seen. The dreams weren't just stories — they were warnings. And even if people didn't believe in the prophetic nature of them, they might still feel what she had felt: a strange chill in the bones, a sense of recognition, an echo of something real.

And so she began assembling them — fifteen dreams in total — into what would become her first and only major work of prophecy: *The Future I Saw.*

The process wasn't easy. Ryo had to revisit dreams that had shaken her deeply, sometimes ones she hadn't thought about in years. She reopened pages of old journals, many yellowed and worn, flipping through her own handwriting and rough sketches. Some drawings brought back the emotions with shocking intensity. She remembered the nights she'd woken up sweating. The mornings she'd sat at her desk before sunrise, desperately sketching the visions before they faded.

Translating these raw experiences into a manga format meant more than just cleaning up the drawings — it meant reimagining how they could be shared with a reader who hadn't lived through the dream with her. Each panel had to carry both the clarity and the ambiguity of the original experience. She didn't want to explain the dreams too much. They weren't puzzles to be solved. They were messages to be witnessed.

The art in *The Future I Saw* is sparse but precise. Dreamlike, yes, but grounded. She avoided flashy stylization in favor of simple, emotive imagery. It wasn't about impressing manga fans. It was about telling the truth. She often drew herself as a character — not heroic or dramatic, just as she was: a quiet observer trying to make sense of what she'd seen.

Each of the fifteen dreams selected for the book carried a timestamp. A date she had the dream. And where possible, she included what happened in the real world afterward. Not all of the events had come true by the time of publication in 1999. Some were still in the uncertain category — those eerie visions that had not yet aligned with anything recognizable. Others, however, had already come to pass.

One of the most haunting inclusions was her dream of the 1995 Kobe earthquake. She had drawn it in the early 1980s and left it untouched for over a decade. The sketch showed collapsing buildings, chaos in the streets, and a date scrawled in the corner. When the actual disaster hit and the images on the news mirrored what she had once seen in her sleep, she knew that sketch had to be included.

Another entry was her vision of Princess Diana's death. It wasn't graphic, but it carried the emotional weight of grief, loss, and global mourning. A quiet dream, one that left her heavy when she woke. She had drawn it years before 1997. When the world lost Diana, she returned to the dream with a shiver, realizing just how close it had been.

And then there was the dream that continues to haunt readers: a catastrophic event marked with the date *July 2025*. In the manga, it's depicted with rising water, mass displacement, and a haunting figure — an old man — who seems to observe from the edge of the scene. The significance of the old man is never explained. Ryo didn't try to interpret it. She just drew what she saw.

Once the artwork and notes were compiled, the next step was publishing — and this, too, was a challenge. The world of manga publishing is competitive and often wary of anything too far outside the mainstream. Editors want fantasy, romance, action. They don't always know what to do with a collection of illustrated dreams that claim to see into the future. But she found a publisher who believed in the work. Maybe not as prophecy, but as something unique. Something worth putting into the world.

The Future I Saw was published in 1999. It was modest in size, not widely distributed, and didn't make a huge splash at first. But it found its audience slowly, like a whispered secret. Readers began to share it. Online forums picked it up. People started comparing the drawings to real-world events. And when, in 2011, the Tōhoku earthquake and tsunami devastated Japan — just as Ryo had described in a dream more than a decade earlier — the book exploded in popularity.

By then, it was no longer a curiosity. It was something chilling. Something that had to be taken seriously.

Ryo never made a follow-up. She never sought to become a public figure or capitalize on the notoriety. In fact, after the publication of *The Future I Saw*, she largely disappeared from public view. The book had done what it needed to do. It spoke for itself. And for those who believed, it became a guide — a haunting map of what was to come.

Looking back, *The Future I Saw* was more than a manga. It was a time capsule. A strange collision between dream and destiny. It remains one of the rare works of art that seems to live outside of time — a book that predicted the world we were heading into, long before we ever arrived.

And it all began with one girl, one dream, and a pencil that wouldn't stop moving.

Dreams That Shook the World

By the time most of the world had heard the name Ryo Tatsuki, it was already too late to call her dreams coincidences. What had started as a private habit — recording vivid, unsettling dreams with pencil and paper — had become something far greater. Her manga *The Future I Saw* might have appeared at first like an oddity, a curious blend of diary and comic, the sort of thing that readers find interesting but forget after the final page. Except, the world didn't forget. Because the world started to catch up to her dreams.

Not long after the book's quiet release in 1999, events began to unfold that mirrored what she had drawn years, sometimes decades, earlier. And each time one of her sketches seemed to align with a real-world catastrophe, her work gained more gravity. People began to dig through the pages of her manga not just as fans of the form, but as investigators — searching for warnings, for patterns, for signs of what might be coming next.

One of the earliest and most talked-about dreams in her collection was her vision of the 1995 Great Hanshin Earthquake. She had seen it in her sleep nearly 15 years before it happened. In the dream, the city was breaking apart — buildings falling, streets cracking, people running. She didn't know the exact city in the vision at the time, but the imagery was precise. When the earthquake hit Kobe and over 6,000 lives were lost, people began looking back at her sketch and realizing just how eerily accurate it had been. The dream had taken place in 1982. The earthquake came in 1995. The drawing was timestamped. And the resemblance was impossible to ignore.

Then came her dream of Princess Diana. It was not a nightmare filled with flames or death — it was more symbolic, somber. A woman being followed, overwhelmed by pressure, disappearing into a tunnel. She drew it without knowing who the woman was. Later, in 1997, when Diana died in a car crash in a tunnel in Paris, the dream came back to her like a ghost. She didn't publicize it. But the drawing was there, quietly waiting.

Even more haunting was her vision of Freddie Mercury. In one of her dreams, she saw a man singing passionately, but something about him was fading. In the sketch she made later, he looked strong yet weary, as if his energy was burning out from within. At the time, she didn't even know who he was. When Mercury died in 1991 after a long illness he had kept hidden, her drawing took on new meaning. The emotions in it weren't just artistic guesses. They captured a private pain, one that had not yet been made public when she had her vision.

But the dream that truly shook the world — the one that changed everything — came in 1991. She saw herself watching a giant wave crash over buildings. The ocean was in the wrong place, swallowing streets and people alike. The sky was dark, filled with screaming birds and shattered glass. The date she saw was March 11, though the year was unclear. She drew it, noted the dream, and moved on. It wasn't until two decades later that the significance of that dream hit with full force.

On March 11, 2011, Japan was struck by the most powerful earthquake in its recorded history. The resulting tsunami devastated entire towns along the coast, took over 18,000 lives, and triggered a nuclear meltdown in Fukushima. When people revisited *The Future I Saw*, they found the drawing. They saw the date. They saw the wave. And suddenly, Ryo Tatsuki wasn't just a manga artist anymore. She was something else.

Her name began trending. News outlets revisited her book. Copies of *The Future I Saw* that had once collected dust on shelves were now being sold at auctions for thousands of dollars. Some readers were shaken. Others were obsessed. And a few dismissed it all as clever post-event interpretation. But the dates didn't lie. The sketches had existed long before the events they resembled.

In the middle of this storm of interest, Ryo did something unexpected. She didn't step into the spotlight. She didn't give interviews or appear on talk shows. She remained largely silent. Maybe it was humility. Maybe it was fear. Or maybe she simply understood the weight of what she had been seeing all along — that this wasn't entertainment. These were glimpses of something real. And the more people believed, the heavier that responsibility became.

What set her apart from others who claimed to have prophetic visions was the quiet clarity of her work. She didn't make loud predictions or try to profit from fear. She didn't build a following or claim divine insight. She simply drew. She let the images speak for themselves. That's what made the world take her seriously. Her drawings were dated, detailed, and impossible to dismiss as accidents.

Of course, not every dream in her collection has come true — not yet. Some remain mysterious. Unmatched. Maybe they are symbolic. Maybe they represent events still to come. Or maybe some futures were only possibilities, avoided or altered by choices the world made along the way. But as time passed, one dream began to rise in the collective imagination: her vision of July 2025.

In the sketch, there's a scene of devastation — a towering wall of water, people running, cities drowning. At the edge of the chaos stands an old man with a long beard, watching in silence. Ryo has never claimed to know what this vision means. She only documented what she saw. But the date — July 5, 2025 — is now etched in the minds of her readers, many of whom are quietly waiting, hoping that this is one vision that doesn't come true.

And yet, even if it does not, the significance of her work remains. Ryo Tatsuki didn't just shake the world with her dreams. She forced it to reconsider what dreams could be. Are they echoes from the future? Warnings? Subconscious truths that defy explanation? Or simply art that dances dangerously close to reality?

Whatever the answer, one thing is certain: Ryo's dreams changed the way we think about time, memory, and what it means to witness the future before it happens.

The world may not yet understand her. But the world is listening now.

Kobe Earthquake Foretold

The Kobe Earthquake is remembered in Japan as one of the most devastating natural disasters of the twentieth century. But for Ryo Tatsuki, it was something else as well. It was the moment her dreams crossed a line — from private experiences she had recorded in silence, to real-world phenomena she had seen before they ever occurred. It was the moment her subconscious and the physical world met in an eerie, undeniable collision.

In her dream, which she had sometime in 1982, she was standing in the middle of a city street. It was early morning. The sky was a dull gray, almost metallic, and the air had a strange density to it — heavy, expectant. Then the trembling began. At first it was subtle, like distant thunder, but it quickly grew violent. Buildings cracked open as if an invisible hand had gripped their foundations and twisted them. Concrete fell like rain. The roads opened up. There were screams, fires, the howling of car alarms, and then silence. Ryo remembered looking at a newspaper on the ground in her dream. On it, in black smudged ink, was the year: 1995.

She woke up sweating, her heart hammering, her breath shallow. She immediately wrote the dream down and drew the image that haunted her the most — a building split at the corner, leaning into another like a wounded animal, a broken power line hanging down, and people running in one direction while others stood frozen, unsure which way was safe. She dated the sketch: 1982. She wrote beneath it: "Dream. City. Earthquake. 1995?"

For years, it was just another entry in her growing dream archive. She had no idea what city she had seen. No reason to believe it was Kobe. Japan, after all, is no stranger to earthquakes. But the clarity of the dream, and the eerie presence of the date, stuck with her. She didn't share it with anyone. Who would listen? Who would believe her? Even she didn't know what to make of it. So she did what she always did. She recorded it, drew it, and let it be.

Then came the morning of January 17, 1995.

At 5:46 AM, the Great Hanshin Earthquake struck the Hyōgo Prefecture, with its epicenter beneath the northern part of Awaji Island. It was powerful, registering 7.3 on the Richter scale, and lasted only about 20 seconds — but that was enough to reduce parts of Kobe to rubble. Over 6,400 people were killed, more than 300,000 displaced, and a major urban region was left shattered.

Ryo, like the rest of Japan, watched the horror unfold on the television news. But unlike most viewers, she wasn't just witnessing a catastrophe. She was remembering it.

She rushed to her old notebooks, flipping through the pages until she found the sketch from over a decade earlier. It was all there. The collapsed building. The splintered street. The stunned people, unsure which way to run. And the date — 1995 — staring back at her like a warning from her younger self.

What had once been a strange and solitary experience became, in an instant, something entirely different. It wasn't just a dream. It was a prophecy. And it had come true with disturbing precision.

But Ryo didn't go public. She didn't send the sketch to the newspapers or announce it on television. That wasn't her nature. She was still just an artist — a manga creator with a strange connection to her dreams. She wasn't looking for fame or validation. She was trying to understand what this meant, and whether it was going to keep happening.

Still, the Kobe earthquake marked a shift. It was the first time a real event had aligned so exactly with one of her dreams — down to the year. After that, she began taking her documentation even more seriously. She no longer doubted the value of what she was seeing. Whether or not anyone else believed in it, she had to continue recording. Because the dream about Kobe wasn't the only one that had felt real. And if that one had come true, others might too.

She began going back through her sketches, organizing them, dating them, analyzing the imagery for hidden meanings. She noticed certain patterns — recurring landscapes, repeating symbols, strange figures that showed up more than once. She didn't always know what they meant. But she understood that they were important.

Eventually, the Kobe earthquake dream — and others like it — would become the foundation for *The Future I Saw*, her 1999 manga that compiled fifteen of her most powerful dreams. And it was that dream of Kobe, drawn in 1982, which gave the book its haunting credibility.

When readers later discovered that she had recorded the dream of the 1995 earthquake more than a decade before it happened, interest in her work surged. Her manga wasn't just another artistic curiosity. It was a document. A potential warning system. Or, depending on your perspective, a message from some deeper layer of time.

To this day, the Kobe dream remains one of the clearest and most chilling examples of Ryo Tatsuki's abilities. It didn't predict every detail — no dream ever could — but it caught something essential. The feeling of panic. The exact type of destruction. The sense of being present inside a moment that hadn't yet occurred. It wasn't the kind of thing you could fake. And it wasn't the kind of thing you could ignore.

So the world began to watch her. Not as a celebrity, but as a quiet, almost reluctant oracle — one who never asked to be one. Ryo simply continued doing what she had always done. She drew. She dreamed. And she waited.

The Kobe Earthquake showed her, and everyone else, that the future wasn't always a mystery. Sometimes it visited you in your sleep. Sometimes it whispered to you in a language only your pencil could understand.

Princess Diana: A Premonition

The dream came to Ryo Tatsuki in the early 1990s. It was quiet and strange — not the kind of violent, visually explosive vision she sometimes had of earthquakes or floods, but something softer, more intimate, and yet undeniably tragic. In the dream, she was walking through a dimly lit tunnel. The walls curved overhead like the inside of a cocoon, echoing with silence. Then she saw a woman standing alone beneath a single, cold light. Elegant, tall, and graceful, the woman had an aura of sadness around her, like someone carrying the weight of the world on her shoulders. People surrounded her — photographers, mostly — but they weren't speaking. Just watching. Flashbulbs going off like small bursts of lightning.

Ryo didn't know who the woman was. She couldn't see her face clearly, but she sensed the importance of her presence. The woman turned her head as if hearing something distant, and then everything shifted. There was a roar, a flash, and then stillness. Ryo remembered waking up feeling an intense grief she couldn't explain. Her heart ached in a way that felt physical. She didn't even cry, because it wasn't sadness in the typical sense — it was the residue of something heavy. A kind of mourning.

She did what she always did: she sketched it. The tunnel. The woman. The light. The sense of being watched and followed. She drew it exactly as she remembered, and below the image she wrote the words that had repeated in her head when she awoke: "She didn't want to be seen, but the world wouldn't look away." She dated the sketch and filed it away with the others. It didn't make much sense. Not then.

Fast-forward a few years. It was the end of August, 1997. The world was stunned by the sudden news: Princess Diana had died in a car crash in Paris. The details were surreal. A high-speed chase. A Mercedes-Benz. A tunnel. Paparazzi. A world icon gone in an instant. When Ryo saw the news, she froze. It wasn't just the image of the tunnel or the involvement of photographers — it was the *feeling*. That exact same aura of sorrow, of quiet beauty, of vulnerability that had haunted her years earlier.

She went back to her sketch. The resemblance wasn't literal — Diana's face wasn't in the dream — but symbolically, it was undeniable. Ryo hadn't known who the woman was in the dream, but now she understood. It had been Diana.

There was a particular image that struck Ryo more than any other: the haunting notion that Diana, even in death, had been seen by millions, and yet had remained emotionally misunderstood. That mirrored the dream perfectly. The woman standing under the light — visible, watched, and yet tragically alone.

Unlike other dreams she'd had, Ryo didn't publicize this one. She didn't share it immediately or try to convince anyone it had meaning. But she knew what it had been. It was a premonition. Another window into an approaching moment. Another encounter with a future that hadn't yet arrived when she'd first dreamed it.

What made it all the more unsettling was how subtle the dream had been. No obvious symbols of death. No loud voice announcing fate. It was just atmosphere. Symbolism. A tone. But Ryo had learned by then that these were the dreams that often mattered most. The quiet ones. The ones that didn't scream disaster but whispered of inevitability.

When she eventually included the dream in *The Future I Saw*, she didn't over-explain it. That wasn't her way. She simply told the reader the date of the dream, what she saw, and how it felt. The rest was up to interpretation. Some readers shrugged it off. Others were deeply moved. There were always those who saw connections in her work only after the fact, and others who accused her of fitting drawings to headlines. But the dream had been sketched and dated well before August 31, 1997. That was indisputable.

And what lingered with her wasn't the accuracy. It was the ache.

Ryo often said that she didn't *want* to be right. Her dreams weren't triumphs. They were burdens. Each time something she had drawn came to pass, it didn't fill her with pride — it filled her with unease. The sketch of the unknown woman in the tunnel had stayed with her because it wasn't about disaster on a mass scale. It was personal. Human. One life, precious and lost.

It reminded her, too, that her dreams didn't always show large-scale calamities. Sometimes they revealed heartbreak. Sometimes they revealed moments that would fracture the soul of the world in quieter ways. Diana's death was one of those moments. It wasn't just the loss of a person — it was the end of an era, the shattering of an illusion, the collective grief of millions who felt like they knew her.

Ryo, in her own quiet way, had already grieved — years before the rest of us even knew we needed to.

She would never meet Diana. She would never speak of the dream in public speeches or claim credit for its eerie resemblance to real events. But in the privacy of her dream journal, the sketch remained. A woman beneath a light. A tunnel full of silence. The knowing weight of being seen.

It was not a prediction, in the loud and theatrical sense. It was a moment — felt, recorded, and remembered.

And like so many of Ryo Tatsuki's dreams, it arrived softly... just before everything changed.

Freddie Mercury's Final Note

Ryo Tatsuki had never been a particular fan of Queen. She didn't dislike the music — it simply hadn't been a dominant presence in her life. Western music, while not unfamiliar to her, was just something that floated in the background of cafés and department stores. So when she dreamed of a man she didn't recognize, singing in a room full of light and sorrow, she didn't assign it much meaning at first. It was one of those dreams that left a strange feeling behind, but without context, it became just another entry in her growing collection.

The dream occurred sometime in 1986. In it, Ryo found herself watching a performance that felt more like a farewell than a concert. The man on stage stood alone beneath a soft spotlight, singing with a passion that felt too large for the room. His voice wasn't just strong — it was *aching*. As he sang, he seemed to grow smaller, as though the song was pulling something vital from him. There were no instruments, no crowd — just him, surrounded by white space. And yet, Ryo could feel that millions of people were somehow watching. Mourning. Celebrating. All at once.

In her dream journal, she drew the man. High cheekbones, a sharp jawline, intense eyes. His mouth open mid-note. She added a note in the corner: "He sings like it's the last thing he'll ever do." The image stayed with her for weeks.

She didn't know who he was, but she sensed that he was real. And that he was fading.

She filed the dream away, like so many others, and went on with her life.

Years later, in 1991, news of Freddie Mercury's death began to ripple across the world. Lead vocalist of Queen. A rock icon. One of the greatest voices of his generation. He had passed away quietly, only a day after publicly revealing he had been battling AIDS. For many, the loss felt like a sudden storm — shocking, irreversible, and far too soon. But for Ryo, something stirred. The image from her dream returned with startling clarity. The man in the spotlight. The voice. The expression of power and vulnerability blended into one.

She searched through her dream sketches until she found the drawing from five years earlier. The face wasn't a perfect match, but the energy — the feeling — was unmistakable. This had been him. The performance without an audience. The song that felt like a goodbye. The unshakable sense that the man was giving everything he had left.

In hindsight, Ryo came to believe that she had seen Mercury not in his death, but in the emotional essence of it. The final note. The last echo of a voice that had carried millions. It wasn't a vision of his passing in the literal sense — there were no hospital beds, no funerals. It was his presence distilled into a symbol. And perhaps that was why it had come to her the way it did. Because even in his final days, Freddie Mercury was more than a man. He was a sound. A feeling. A final note that lingered in the air.

Ryo chose to include this dream in *The Future I Saw* not because she wanted recognition, but because it marked something different from her usual visions. It wasn't a disaster. It wasn't mass tragedy. It was personal. And it showed her that even the deaths of individuals, when felt deeply by the world, carried their own kind of seismic weight.

The drawing in her book is gentle. A man in a white room. A microphone suspended in front of him like a relic. No caption beyond the date of the dream: 1986. And the moment of realization: 1991.

Readers of the manga who saw that panel were struck not just by the timing, but by the tone. This wasn't a prophecy drenched in fear. It was tender. Honest. It conveyed love, loss, and legacy — everything Mercury embodied in his final years. For those who had loved his music, it felt like a tribute from someone who never knew him, but somehow felt what he was going through.

Ryo often said that some dreams came to her with sharp clarity, while others were cloaked in metaphor. This one, she believed, had been an emotional truth more than a literal one. She hadn't seen Mercury's face because it wasn't about him as a person — it was about his *impact*. His exit. His echo.

What struck her the most in retrospect was how the dream captured the dignity of someone giving the world one last performance, even if no one else was in the room. That image haunted her — not with sadness, but with reverence. It was the kind of dream that didn't scream for attention, but whispered a farewell across time.

Freddie Mercury's final note wasn't a chord or a sound. It was a presence. A soul. A vibration. And in some inexplicable way, Ryo Tatsuki had tuned into it before the world even knew he was slipping away.

Another dream. Another drawing. Another truth waiting to be understood.

The 2011 Tsunami: A Predicted Tragedy

If there is one dream that changed everything for Ryo Tatsuki — not just in how her work was viewed, but in how the world began to perceive the boundary between dreams and reality — it was the one dated March 11. A dream she had long before the year 2011. A dream that seemed, at the time, like a surreal nightmare with too much water, too much chaos, and too much emotion to ever feel real. But it *did* become real. Tragically real. And it was that horrifying synchronicity that elevated Ryo from a curious manga artist to something much more mysterious — an accidental oracle, a reluctant prophet.

The dream came to her in 1996. She remembered it vividly because the sensation of drowning, of being swallowed by the ocean, lingered in her body even hours after she woke. In it, she stood on a coastline — not tropical, not warm — but somewhere distinctly Japanese. It felt cold, grey, the sky heavy with clouds. Then, without warning, the sea rose up in silence. There was no dramatic sound effect, no roaring wave. Just a sudden and horrifying realization that water was advancing, and no one could outrun it.

She saw cars tumbling over each other like toys. People screaming. Entire houses lifting from their foundations and floating inland as if gravity had forgotten its job. The most disturbing part was how slowly it seemed to move in the dream — not fast like a crashing wave, but steady and unstoppable, as if the sea itself had decided to walk onto land.

She woke gasping for air.

As she always did, Ryo went to her desk and drew the vision. A quiet town being engulfed by the ocean. A woman standing on a rooftop holding a child. A date circled in the margin: March 11. There was no year attached. Just the number. She didn't understand it then. It was another one of many sketches — strange, haunting, but unsolved. Like so many other drawings in her journals, it went into a folder and stayed there, waiting.

Fifteen years passed.

On the morning of March 11, 2011, Japan experienced one of the most devastating natural disasters in its history. At 2:46 PM local time, a magnitude 9.0 earthquake struck off the northeastern coast, triggering a colossal tsunami that struck the Tōhoku region with unimaginable force. Towns were swept away. Nearly 20,000 people were killed. Entire communities were erased from the map.

And not long after the wave receded, people began to remember something else — that an obscure manga artist named Ryo Tatsuki had once drawn a tsunami scene with that exact date.

Word spread fast. Copies of *The Future I Saw* were suddenly in high demand. Readers, journalists, and even scientists began flipping through the pages, hunting for clues, trying to verify the claims. The panel was there. The water. The chaos. The rooftops. The unmistakable grief. And in the margin — that quiet but chilling date: March 11.

She had drawn it fifteen years before the wave struck.

What made the prediction so jarring wasn't just the accuracy of the destruction — it was the emotional tone. The drawing didn't depict spectacle. It captured fear, despair, helplessness. It felt human. Real. And that was what separated it from coincidence. Ryo hadn't just dreamed of a tsunami — she had *felt* it, years before it happened.

Suddenly, her work wasn't just manga. It was evidence.

The world took notice. Some dismissed it as clever retroactive editing, but those who knew her work confirmed the date had been written long before 2011. Others called it a warning that had gone unheeded. And many, especially in Japan, treated it as something sacred — a message from somewhere beyond ordinary time, drawn by a woman who never sought fame or attention for what she saw in her sleep.

Ryo, for her part, remained quiet. She didn't make television appearances. She didn't use the attention to promote herself. She let the work speak. But friends said the disaster weighed heavily on her. She had seen it coming — not in precise detail, but in emotional reality — and she had not known what to do with that knowledge. How could she have known it was a real future? How could anyone have known?

The drawing from 1996 is now one of the most well-known pieces from *The Future I Saw*. It has been shared widely across the internet. Some keep a copy of it taped inside their homes. Some believe it marks her as a true visionary. And some still struggle with the implications. What does it mean to see the future but not understand it until it's too late?

This dream, more than any other, forced people to confront the possibility that time may not be as linear as we believe. That some part of the mind — perhaps during sleep — has access to things we cannot comprehend. Ryo never claimed to understand why she had these dreams. She never branded herself as psychic. She never claimed to see all futures. Only that she had them, she drew them, and they stayed with her long after the rest of the world had forgotten.

The 2011 tsunami was a national wound. A collective trauma. But in the quiet corners of manga shops and internet forums, it was also something else: a validation of a strange little book published years before. A dream once laughed off, suddenly seen in a new and sobering light.

And Ryo? She remained in the background, sketching, dreaming, documenting. Because that's what she had always done.

The sea came for the land, and the land was not ready.

But Ryo had seen it. And she tried to tell us — in pencil, in silence, on a page.

The Virus of 2020: Foreseen

By the time the world entered the year 2020, Ryo Tatsuki had long since retreated from public life. Her name was still spoken in quiet reverence in certain circles — among manga enthusiasts, paranormal researchers, and those who followed the rhythm of her strange prophetic dreams — but she was not part of the mainstream. *The Future I Saw* had become a cult artifact, especially after the tsunami prediction shook belief systems. Still, it wasn't until a new kind of invisible catastrophe swept across the world that readers would return to her work with fresh eyes — and a familiar sense of dread.

The dream that would later be linked to the global pandemic came to her in 1995. At the time, she didn't fully grasp what it meant. It wasn't violent. It wasn't filled with natural disasters or collapsing buildings like so many of her more vivid nightmares. It was different. Still. Silent. Almost suffocating. In it, she walked through a city that felt hauntingly empty. Streets that should've been full of people were abandoned. Storefronts were shuttered. Trains sat idle. And the faces of those few who passed her were covered. Everyone wore masks — not as a fashion or to block out pollution, but with an eerie sense of fear.

In the dream, she found herself trying to speak to someone, but her voice wouldn't come. The person stepped back as if scared of her. There were no screams, no alarms — just distance. A heavy sense of distance. And over everything, a strange floating word: "quarantine." She didn't even know if she'd heard that word in real life yet. It was written in kanji in her dream — self-isolation. There were also numbers, vague and flickering, like time on a broken clock. One of them stood out: "2020."

When she woke, she wrote it all down. She drew the empty street, the masked passers-by, the sterile sense of anxiety in the air. She labeled the page with the words "Sickness Dream – 2020?" and moved on. At the time, it felt too abstract to dwell on. Illness was always part of human life, and Japan was no stranger to mask-wearing, especially during flu season. But there was something deeper in that dream. Something more chilling. Not a sickness of the body, exactly — but of society.

It wasn't until early 2020, as reports of a novel coronavirus began to dominate the headlines, that people started returning to her manga. In particular, one panel stood out: a masked crowd walking through a downtown cityscape, all distanced from each other, and above them, the phrase: "a sickness spreads quietly." At the time of publication in *The Future I Saw*, no one thought much of it. It seemed like an artistic metaphor. A symbolic dream. But in hindsight, it felt disturbingly specific.

As the pandemic worsened, readers began connecting the dots. The empty streets. The masks. The fear of being near another person. The strange aura of social paralysis. And the date: 2020. It had all been there, drawn and printed years earlier. Once again, the internet caught fire with speculation. Blogs, forums, and videos poured over her work, scanning for any other clues. Was it possible she had seen the global lockdowns coming decades in advance? And if so, what else had she seen?

The panel wasn't a prediction in the traditional sense. Ryo hadn't written "a global virus will shut down the world." She hadn't named it. She hadn't sketched hospitals or world leaders. But the atmosphere — the emotional *tone* of the dream — matched what millions were now living through. And that, more than the details, was what always made Ryo's dreams so potent. She didn't document facts. She documented *feelings*. And those feelings often turned out to be painfully accurate.

During the early days of the pandemic, interest in her work spiked once more. Digital copies of *The Future I Saw* circulated widely. People began treating her drawings as a strange sort of guidance — not because they could stop anything, but because they made people feel like someone, somewhere, had seen this coming. That we weren't entirely blind.

Ryo, however, did not come forward. She didn't release a new book. She didn't offer updates. There were rumours she had drawn more recent dreams but hadn't shared them publicly. Others speculated she had gone silent because she didn't want to alarm anyone. Perhaps she feared what else might come true.

There's something deeply unsettling about a dream from 1995 capturing the essence of a world event twenty-five years later. Especially when that dream was never meant to scare — just to record. It invites big questions: What are dreams really made of? Can the subconscious tap into time? Are there people like Ryo who somehow — inexplicably — are tuned in to future frequencies?

Skeptics, of course, tried to disprove the whole thing. They pointed out that masks were part of Japanese culture long before COVID. That empty streets could symbolize anything. That dreams are notoriously vague and easily bent to fit almost any event. But even some of the skeptics had to pause when they saw the date: 2020. And the quiet panic in the drawing. It didn't feel like a metaphor anymore. It felt like a whisper from the future.

In a world desperate for answers and patterns, Ryo's work became a sort of mirror. Not to explain what was happening — but to reflect what had always been quietly waiting in the shadows.

The virus changed the world. It altered how we live, how we connect, how we think. But for Ryo Tatsuki, it was another confirmation that dreams are not always figments of imagination. Sometimes they are early warnings. Echoes. Signals. Sometimes, they are truth before it becomes reality.

And long before the headlines, long before the lockdowns, long before the fear settled over the planet like a silent fog, Ryo had already seen us there — walking the same streets, keeping our distance, wondering what would happen next.

The Unpublished Dreams

While *The Future I Saw* revealed fifteen of Ryo Tatsuki's most vivid and significant prophetic dreams, it only scratched the surface of what she had actually seen. For every dream that made it into the pages of her manga, there were dozens — maybe hundreds — that never saw the light of day. These were her unpublished dreams, the fragments and flashes, the visions too personal, too confusing, or too terrifying to share publicly. And yet, they may hold just as much weight as the ones the world knows.

Ryo never stopped dreaming. Even after her book was published, even after she began to gain attention from the most unexpected corners of the world, the dreams kept coming. Sometimes they arrived in clusters, weeks of recurring themes and symbols. Other times, they came in isolated bursts — a single image, a word, a sensation that lingered long enough to be sketched and recorded. She documented them with the same quiet discipline she always had. Her notebooks multiplied. Her sketches continued. But she never rushed to publish them. There was something sacred, perhaps even dangerous, about sharing them too freely.

Many of these dreams remained hidden in her studio, stacked in files, sketched on napkins, scrawled in the margins of personal journals. Only a handful of people close to her were aware of just how many she had recorded. Some of them were simply too vague to be useful. A dream of a black sun rising over a desert — what did that mean? A feeling of suffocation in a metallic room filled with television screens — a metaphor? A warning? Even Ryo herself didn't always know.

And that was part of why she withheld so many. She believed in the importance of recording everything, but she did not believe in publishing for shock value or fame. She never wanted to be sensational. If a dream didn't speak clearly to her, or didn't carry that heavy, uncanny sensation she had come to recognize in her most prophetic visions, she left it alone.

But that didn't mean the dreams were forgotten.

There are sketches she drew in the early 2000s that have become sources of speculation among her most devoted followers. One dream reportedly featured an underground city filled with silent people wearing silver armbands, staring at a black monolith. Another involved a digital storm, where all screens in the world went blank and then flickered with a single message: "You were warned." No date. No explanation. Just raw imagery. Dreams like these have never been seen by the public, but their descriptions have circulated quietly among those who knew her or who had seen her private sketches.

Some of the unpublished dreams seemed oddly mundane. A tree growing through the middle of a freeway. A clock tower that melted every time someone looked at it. A field of glass birds buried under snow. These weren't predictions, at least not obviously. But Ryo had learned not to judge a dream by how dramatic it appeared. Some of her most accurate visions had come dressed in quiet symbolism.

Then there were the dreams she reportedly refused to draw. Ones that disturbed her so much that she couldn't bring herself to capture them in pencil. In one, she was walking through a hospital where the patients weren't ill — they were paralysed in time, frozen mid-motion. In another, she saw the ocean burning, but no one around her noticed. They went about their daily lives as the flames crept closer.

She shared some of these verbally with close friends, but they were never included in her book. Part of her hesitation, perhaps, came from a sense of emotional exhaustion. Dreaming the future wasn't something she could control, and the pressure to interpret and explain what she saw had begun to wear on her. She didn't want to be the center of conspiracy theories or become a permanent target of skepticism and media attention.

There's also the possibility that some dreams simply felt *too soon*. Ryo may have sensed that the world wasn't ready for what she had seen. After all, when she first released *The Future I Saw*, it didn't make headlines. People only took notice when reality caught up with the drawings. If she had published visions of an unknown city vanishing beneath the ground, or skies filled with artificial stars, it may have seemed like science fiction — or madness. But she knew better than most how quickly the improbable could become real.

It's also been whispered that in some of her unpublished notes, there are references to years not yet reached. 2026. 2031. Even 2040. No clear events are listed, only feelings: "a fall," "black winter," "mass forgetting." The vagueness only adds to the mystery. Were these random, or were they glimpses of futures still on the horizon?

What makes the unpublished dreams so haunting is precisely their ambiguity. They suggest a deeper layer to Ryo's experience — one that the public never fully saw. While *The Future I Saw* provided a curated glimpse into her gift, the rest of her dream archive remains unknown, locked away in sketchbooks and memory, waiting.

And perhaps that's the way she intended it.

Ryo never saw herself as a prophet. She didn't want followers or believers. She didn't claim to see every future, or even to understand the ones she glimpsed. She was, at heart, an artist — a dreamer with a pencil and an uncanny ability to witness what others couldn't. The unpublished dreams, then, aren't failures or discarded visions. They are reminders of the mystery that surrounded her. A part of the story we were never meant to fully know.

But for those who have seen the truth in her pages — those who lived through the disasters she once dreamed — the idea of hundreds more unpublished drawings quietly sitting in the dark is both terrifying and awe-inspiring.

What else did Ryo Tatsuki see?

And more importantly... what has yet to come true?

The Complete Version: Revisiting the Past

By the time *The Future I Saw* had become the quiet phenomenon it was always destined to be, a new conversation had already begun to emerge — not about what the book contained, but what it *didn't*. The original manga, first published in 1999, included fifteen of Ryo Tatsuki's most vivid dreams. It was slim, restrained, and careful in its tone, never sensational, never overreaching. But over the years, especially after the 2011 tsunami dream came true, readers began asking the inevitable question: was there more?

The answer, as it turned out, was yes.

For over a decade, *The Future I Saw* existed as a strange collector's item. A whisper of a book that surfaced in online forums, UFO conventions, spiritualist bookstores, and fringe media outlets. But as more and more of her dreams appeared to echo real-world events, interest swelled. Eventually, a complete edition was re-released — with additional content, commentary, and newly included dreams that had never made it into the original print. This new version was still understated in its presentation, but to those who had followed her work from the beginning, it was monumental. It meant Ryo Tatsuki had returned, at least in spirit, to offer more of what she'd seen.

Revisiting the past, for her, was not just about updating a book. It was a delicate emotional journey. Each drawing carried a weight. Each dream came wrapped in the context of when she'd seen it — and who she was at the time. Many of the new pages in the complete edition weren't new drawings, but old sketches finally ready to be shared. They had lived quietly in her archives for decades, waiting for the right moment.

Among the most notable inclusions was her expanded vision of the 2011 tsunami. In the original version, the dream was already chilling, but in the complete edition, she revealed additional panels that had never been published — scenes of people evacuating, of animals fleeing inland, of digital clocks all showing the same moment before going dark. She hadn't known what to make of those symbols back then, but they carried more meaning after the fact. Time frozen. Warnings ignored. Nature reclaiming what humans believed was theirs.

Another newly added dream — one not linked to any known disaster — depicted a city surrounded by mirrors, all reflecting a sun that wasn't in the sky. The meaning was unclear, but the accompanying date scrawled in the corner — "2025?" — renewed public speculation about what she had seen, and whether it might relate to the mysterious July 5, 2025, dream already revealed in her original manga.

What made this complete version so compelling wasn't just the dreams themselves, but the act of *returning* to them. Ryo didn't revise her work to fit headlines. She didn't redraw anything. The original sketches remained untouched. What she offered instead was context — brief notes on how the dreams felt in hindsight, what she remembered from the nights they occurred, and how she interpreted them *now* versus then.

One such note was written beneath a drawing of a city skyline split by a glowing fissure. She had originally drawn it in 1991. In the complete edition, she added a comment: "It didn't come in the form I expected, but something broke. Something under the surface." She didn't say more. She didn't need to.

Revisiting the past was not an act of validation for Ryo — it was an act of preservation. She understood that many readers had come to her work not just looking for predictions, but for meaning. For a sense that someone, somewhere, had seen this chaos coming and tried, in the quietest way, to prepare us for it. She wasn't offering answers. She was offering breadcrumbs. A map made of instinct and ink.

The complete version also offered space to reflect on dreams that hadn't come true — yet. She didn't shy away from those. Several sketches remained deeply mysterious, such as the vision of a "cracking sky" over Tokyo, or the dream of a "silent eclipse" witnessed by people in silver robes. These hadn't materialized. Not in any literal way. But she left them in, with a note: "Not every dream is meant to be understood at the time it is drawn."

For readers, this transparency only deepened the mystique. Ryo wasn't claiming to see all things. She wasn't pretending to have a perfect track record. She simply continued to do what she always had — record what she saw in sleep, and trust that the meaning would arrive later, if it was meant to.

Perhaps the most poignant addition to the complete edition was a final page, simple and unillustrated. Just a line of text written in her distinctive, small handwriting: *"If nothing else, I hope these dreams remind you to pay attention."*

That's what it had always been about. Not fear. Not fame. But awareness. Attunement. A subtle invitation to listen more closely to the invisible signals around us. To observe. To trust the quiet warnings that come before the storm.

The Future I Saw: Complete Edition was not just a longer book. It was a return. A revisitation of moments that had become, in their own strange way, historical documents. And it reminded everyone who read it that the past is not fixed. That sometimes, dreams are not memories — but messages written backwards across time.

And that maybe, just maybe, the future is already here... we just haven't recognized it yet.

The Symbolism in Her Art

For all the unsettling accuracy of Ryo Tatsuki's prophetic dreams, one of the most mysterious and mesmerizing aspects of her work lies in the layers of symbolism she embedded in her art — whether consciously or not. Unlike a typical manga artist driven by narrative structure or genre conventions, Ryo drew images from a place that existed somewhere between the conscious and subconscious, between waking reality and the quiet currents of her dreams. What emerged from that place wasn't always literal. More often, it was symbolic — images filled with coded meaning, emotional texture, and layered suggestion.

The symbolism in her drawings isn't flashy or cryptic in the way one might expect from apocalyptic or religious visionaries. Her art is restrained, often minimalist, but profoundly evocative. What she chooses to show — or *not* show — in each dream image often carries as much meaning as the date or event it seems to correspond with. In fact, one of the reasons her work continues to captivate new readers is because it leaves so much space for interpretation. Her drawings ask questions rather than offering conclusions.

Take, for example, her famous dream of the 2011 tsunami. While the water and the destruction are evident, what many overlook is the small figure in the bottom right corner — a dog on a rooftop, howling at an empty sky. Ryo never explained that detail, but some believe it symbolizes the raw innocence of life left behind, the silent witness to events humans could not control. Others believe the dog represents loyalty, or perhaps the idea that nature always knows what's coming before we do.

Or consider the dream she had of the 1995 Kobe earthquake. In the foreground of that sketch is a crooked streetlight — barely standing, leaning over the debris. It's not just rubble she focuses on. It's *that* detail. The bent pole, the flickering bulb above chaos. It's a simple image, but one that symbolizes disorientation, loss of structure, and the breakdown of the familiar. The streetlight is something we expect to guide us, to illuminate — and in her dream, it is failing. The message is subtle but undeniable.

Ryo often used environmental symbols to convey the emotional core of her visions. Cracked windows, frayed power lines, shoes left in doorways — all seemingly ordinary objects, yet in her dreams they carry profound weight. A single shoe at the edge of a sidewalk is no longer a random item; it becomes a stand-in for absence, for tragedy, for a life interrupted. These are the details that haunt you after you've turned the page.

Recurring symbols also began to emerge over time. One of the most discussed is the image of the "old man." He appears in several of her dreams, sometimes in the background, sometimes more prominent. He never speaks. He simply observes — always at a distance, often when disaster is about to unfold. Ryo never identified who he was or what he represented, but theories abound. Some say he symbolizes time itself. Others see him as a guide, a witness, or even death personified — not as a reaper, but as a gentle, knowing presence who does not intervene.

Another repeated motif is the circle. It appears in windows, in drawn clocks, in the curvature of waves, even in the sun and moon. Ryo seemed drawn to circular forms — not just because they're natural shapes, but because they represent cycles, returns, the closing and reopening of time. The circle suggests a future that is not linear but spiraling. Events do not simply happen once; they echo, return, evolve.

Color — or rather, the *absence* of it — also plays a symbolic role in her drawings. Most of Ryo's work is in stark black and white, yet within that limited palette, she conveys atmosphere with remarkable precision. When she shades a sky dark in the middle of a dream sequence, it isn't to signal night — it's to reflect a mood. A sense of impending change.

Similarly, when an entire background is left blank, it creates a dreamlike vacuum, isolating the moment and inviting the viewer to project themselves into it.

And then there are the titles she writes beside certain sketches. Often brief and poetic, they act like haiku — not telling, but suggesting. "She stood too still." "We forgot the warning." "This is not the beginning." These captions are part of the symbolism, too. They don't define the drawing, but deepen the mystery. They give the reader just enough to feel something, but not enough to know exactly what it means.

Even dates themselves can be symbolic in her work. Sometimes they are complete — March 11, 2011. Other times, they are fragmented — "July 2025?" or simply a year like "1995." Ryo doesn't always assign certainty to these numbers, and the inclusion of question marks or incomplete dates suggests her own hesitation to draw concrete conclusions. Time, in her art, is as fluid as water. It's a setting, a character, and a warning all at once.

What's most compelling is that Ryo never pretended to understand her own symbolism completely. She didn't offer interpretations. She didn't claim to know what her drawings meant in the grander scheme of things. In that way, she remained honest about her process. The dreams came. She drew them. That was the extent of her role. It was up to others to find meaning — or not.

And perhaps that is what makes her art so enduring. It invites you not just to witness the future, but to reflect on your place within it. Her symbols don't just illustrate a possible tomorrow. They mirror our collective fear, our fragility, our stubborn hope. They ask us to look deeper — not at the obvious, but at the overlooked. The bent pole. The missing shoe. The silent old man.

Because in Ryo Tatsuki's dreams, it is always the quiet details that tell the loudest truth.

The Left Eye: Window to the Past

Among the many recurring motifs and symbolic patterns in Ryo Tatsuki's prophetic dreams and artwork, one of the strangest and most compelling is the presence of a left eye — singular, often disembodied, sometimes embedded into walls, skies, or faces that lack any other detail. It's not the sort of thing you notice at first glance. But once you start looking for it, the left eye appears everywhere. Not both eyes. Not a stylized manga gaze. Just the left.

What could this mean?

Ryo never publicly explained the symbol. In fact, she never even labeled it. But in interviews and handwritten notes included in the extended editions of *The Future I Saw*, she alludes to the left eye more than once, often in cryptic language. In one comment, she writes, *"I saw through the left eye, never the right. That's how I knew it was a memory, not a warning."* Elsewhere, she refers to it simply as "the watcher." She doesn't say who or what it is watching — only that it doesn't look forward. It looks back.

To Ryo, the left eye may have represented the subconscious self. The inner mind. The part of her that wasn't dreaming forward into a possible future but instead absorbing the imprint of what had already occurred — sometimes before she was even born. These visions weren't predictions. They were inheritances. Emotional blueprints of traumas or moments lost to history, surfacing in her dreams like echoes.

She once told a friend that the left eye dreams always felt *older*. Not just in tone or imagery, but in how they lingered after waking. They didn't carry the sharp anxiety of her future dreams, which often jolted her out of sleep. Instead, they brought sorrow, longing, and sometimes a strange sense of déjà vu. As if she were remembering something that didn't belong to her. A collective memory passed down through time.

In one of her more famous unpublished sketches — later released in the complete edition — a child stands before a mirror in an empty house. The mirror reflects the child's face, but only the left eye is visible. The rest of the reflection is a blur. Behind the child is an open door, but it leads not into another room, but into a ruined version of the house itself — crumbling, overgrown, abandoned. The image is chilling. And while Ryo never explained it, the caption beneath reads: *"I don't know this place, but I've lived here before."*

Interpretation varies widely. Some say the left eye represents the human tendency to be haunted by history — both personal and collective. Others argue that in esoteric traditions, the left eye is associated with the Moon, with introspection, with hidden truth. In ancient Egyptian symbolism, for example, the Eye of Horus had both a right and left form — the right eye for the Sun (logic, clarity), and the left for the Moon (intuition, mystery). Ryo may never have studied these traditions directly, but the parallel is difficult to ignore.

In her dreams that focused on events from the past — historical disasters, lost places, even wars — the left eye was often drawn somewhere in the background. In a cracked windowpane. On a billboard half-fallen into the ocean. In the side profile of a figure whose face is mostly erased. And in those images, the atmosphere was never apocalyptic — it was mournful. These weren't warnings. They were *reminders*.

Ryo once said that the left eye dreams felt like they belonged to someone else. She didn't claim ownership of them the way she did with future visions. In fact, she suspected some of them were ancestral — passed down emotionally, if not genetically. Trauma, after all, can live inside families. Events that occur generations before can leave shadows in the subconscious. Ryo's sensitivity to dreams may have made her a vessel for these old echoes — not just future possibilities, but the unprocessed past.

That's why she sometimes referred to the left eye as a "window." It wasn't a spotlight or a camera or even a metaphor for perception. It was a portal through which something else — someone else — looked. Not into the future, but into a time already lived. A portal that opened during sleep, letting fragments through.

One of her most unsettling left-eye dreams involved a city she could never identify — a place with cobblestone streets, horse-drawn carts, and people wearing black veils. In the dream, she was not herself. She was someone else entirely, a man with a limp, watching a fire consume a church. She felt his grief, his guilt. She remembered his name — and it wasn't hers. When she woke up, she couldn't shake the feeling that she'd *been* him. Just for that moment. And of course, when she sketched the scene, a single eye stared from a stained-glass window — the left one.

What all of this suggests is that Ryo wasn't just a dreamer of the future. She was an unconscious historian. Her gift wasn't strictly prophetic — it was liminal. She occupied a space in her sleep where time blurred, and through that blur, she saw what most people forget. Or suppress. Or never even knew.

The left eye, then, isn't just a symbol. It's a signal.

It tells the reader, the viewer, the dreamer: *This already happened.* Maybe not to you. Maybe not in this lifetime. But it happened. And it matters. And someone must remember.

So while the world may know Ryo Tatsuki for her uncanny predictions — the earthquakes, the tsunami, the strange vision of July 2025 — it's worth remembering that half of her dreams weren't about what's coming.

They were about what we've already survived. What we carry. What we must still reckon with.

The left eye sees the past — and in Ryo's hands, it made sure we didn't forget.

The Right Eye: Glimpse into Tomorrow

If the left eye in Ryo Tatsuki's dreams was a window to the past, a portal through which echoes of forgotten tragedies and ancient memories slipped into her sleeping mind, then the right eye was its mirror opposite — a lens that opened just enough to show her the future. A glimpse. A flicker. Never the full picture, never the whole story, but always enough to disturb the stillness of the present.

Among her sketches, it's clear that the right eye carries a different energy. Where the left is often passive, reflective, sorrowful, the right is alert. Focused. Watching from a distance with unsettling clarity. In drawings where a figure has only one eye exposed — and it is the right — the surrounding imagery is often catastrophic or distorted. Something is happening or about to happen, and the eye is not simply witnessing it, but *understanding* it in a way the rest of the world has not yet caught up to.

Ryo never wrote long essays or theories about this duality, but in her handwritten notes, she referred several times to "the eye that knows" and "the eye that sees forward." Unlike the left eye, which carried emotional weight and the residue of things long gone, the right eye seemed to catch a signal from ahead — a mental photograph of something approaching. Her most precise and prophetic dreams always came through this perspective.

She once wrote, *"When the dream begins from the right side, I brace myself."* It was a subtle admission that she knew what kind of dream she was entering even as it started. Not all dreams were equal. Some had the texture of metaphor, emotional processing, or spiritual resonance. But when the vision started with her seeing through the right eye — especially from the perspective of a bird, an outsider, or an impossible camera angle hovering above — that was when she knew she was glimpsing tomorrow.

In one such dream, which she recorded in 1989, she saw an empty highway where every digital sign had gone dark. Above it, satellites hovered lower than they should have. There was a hum in the sky — not a sound, exactly, but a vibration she could feel in her bones. In the foreground, she drew a billboard with one eye in the corner, wide open, staring straight ahead. The right eye. Below it, the words: *"Not yet, but soon."*

This particular drawing wasn't connected to any specific event when she first published it. But after the rise of satellite-based surveillance, digital traffic systems, and the rolling blackouts of the early 2000s, readers began to revisit it. And when people recognized the growing unease around global technological surveillance and loss of privacy, that right eye seemed to grow more chilling by the year. Not because it predicted a date — but because it captured a *direction*.

That was the power of the right eye in Ryo's work. It didn't give answers. It gave trajectory.

In several of her most famous dreams, the right eye appears at a moment of transformation. In her tsunami dream, it's reflected in the water just before the wave crashes. In the July 2025 dream, the old man on the street has only one visible eye — the right — and he's not looking at the chaos unfolding. He's looking past it. Past the flood. Past the buildings. Into something we can't see. Something *beyond*.

It's as if, in Ryo's symbolic language, the right eye doesn't just glimpse the future — it accepts it. It carries none of the sorrow of the left, none of the emotional tethering. The right eye is neutral. Impersonal. It doesn't mourn the future. It observes it.

She once described a dream where she floated above Earth and saw the continents rearranged — not suddenly, but slowly, as if time had sped up. People continued walking through cities that were changing shape beneath them.

Buildings slid apart. Rivers shifted course. In the sky above it all was a blinking light, pulsing with every shift. She drew the dream from the vantage point of the light itself — looking down through a single eye. The right one. When asked about it, she simply said: *"That one came from far away."*

Whether "far away" meant time, space, or something less definable, no one could say. But it echoed a common experience readers had when viewing her work. The sense that the right eye symbolized a vantage point not entirely human — as though someone, or something, was showing her what was coming, and using dreams as a delivery system.

This brings up one of the more provocative theories about Ryo's gift — that she wasn't just dreaming randomly, but was receiving information. That the right eye was not just a symbol, but a *conduit*. A surveillance device not for watching the world as it is, but for scanning what it is becoming. Some followers have gone so far as to suggest that the eye represents artificial intelligence, or even an extra-dimensional consciousness. Ryo never indulged those ideas. She remained grounded, always insisting that she didn't know why she had the dreams — only that she had them.

Still, the symbolism of the right eye continued to appear throughout her unpublished work. Sometimes subtle, sometimes dominant. It became a kind of watermark — an unconscious signal that the dream in question might not be metaphor, but something else. Something precognitive.

In dreams, the mind isn't bound by time the way it is in waking life. And for Ryo, it seemed the right eye was the mind's attempt to make sense of glimpses that arrived uninvited. The symbol of the eye — always singular, never part of a full face — was her shorthand for that disturbing realization: *You are not guessing. You are seeing.*

Her drawings don't scream this message. They whisper it. Through cracked windows. Reflected puddles. Posters peeling off walls. Eyes that are never fully there — just enough to be seen, just enough to be felt.

The left eye remembered. The right eye warned.

And when Ryo drew from the right, the future wasn't a concept anymore. It was a presence. Waiting to unfold. Ready to be seen.

The Old Man in Dreams

Among all the recurring images in Ryo Tatsuki's prophetic dreams, none has sparked more speculation, awe, and quiet unease than the figure of the old man. He is not central in her drawings. He is not explained, labeled, or even addressed directly in *The Future I Saw*. And yet he appears again and again — always at the edges of things, always watching. Always there.

At first, no one noticed him. In the early interpretations of her manga, readers focused on the dramatic content: the tsunami, the crumbling cities, the masks, the flood, the chaos. But it was only after her dreams began to come true that people started looking closer, frame by frame, trying to find hidden meaning in the backgrounds. That's when he started to show up.

Sometimes he stands near a bench. Sometimes behind a window. Sometimes at the far end of a crowd, his face turned just slightly toward the viewer, as if he's aware of being watched — or perhaps he's watching the watcher. He is always bearded, always dressed in an unremarkable coat or robe, and always calm. In fact, his stillness is what makes him so disturbing. While everyone else in Ryo's dream scenes is in motion, reacting to disasters or fleeing from danger, the old man simply stands there, observing.

Ryo never gave him a name. In her original dream notes, she refers to him sparingly and vaguely — once as "the quiet one," and another time as "the one who knew." She never claimed to know who he was. In fact, when pressed in one rare interview about the figure, she simply said, *"He's not a warning. He's a witness."*

That phrase — not a warning, but a witness — carries a strange and powerful weight. In many ways, the old man represents something larger than the disaster unfolding in the frame. He doesn't stop the events. He doesn't interact with the dreamer. He doesn't panic or run. He just watches, quietly, with what some have interpreted as a mix of sorrow and inevitability in his expression.

This leads many to believe that the old man is not a person at all, but a symbol. A manifestation of time, or fate, or even Ryo herself — a part of her subconscious mind watching the moment she's not yet meant to understand. Others go further. They suggest he is a guide, a guardian, or a cosmic recorder — present not to prevent the future, but to witness its arrival and ensure it is remembered.

In one particularly haunting sketch from her unpublished collection, the old man is standing at the base of a collapsed overpass, where cars are stacked like broken toys. In the sky above him is a single, flickering light — some interpret it as a drone, others as a star falling. But what catches the eye is that the man is looking not at the destruction, but at something just out of frame, something the viewer never sees. His right eye is slightly more detailed than the left. The effect is subtle, but it gives the impression that he's aware of something deeper, something *beyond* the dream itself.

It's the consistency of his presence that has made him so important in the mythology surrounding Ryo's work. He shows up in the Kobe earthquake sketch, though few noticed him at first. He is there again in the background of her tsunami dream, standing on the edge of a building as the wave rolls in. He is also present — most disturbingly — in the July 5, 2025 dream. That sketch is infamous now, depicting mass flooding, destruction, and panic. And at the edge of it all, near the vanishing horizon, is the old man, again watching, unmoved.

In that dream, Ryo wrote in the margins: *"He was already there when I arrived."* Which suggests something chilling — that the old man doesn't enter the dream. He's already *in* it, waiting. As if the future is not being dreamed, but visited. And the old man is its only permanent resident.

Some readers have drawn parallels between this figure and cultural archetypes — the hermit in tarot, the prophet in religious texts, the ferryman in mythology. In Jungian terms, he could be seen as a symbol of the "wise old man" archetype, the unconscious mind's representation of deeper knowledge and hidden truth. But Ryo never leaned into any of these explanations. Her drawings don't teach. They record. She leaves the meaning open — the way dreams always do.

There are even those who believe the old man is alive — not metaphorically, but literally. A person who exists in some parallel or future timeline, reaching across dreams to be present at key moments. It's a stretch, perhaps. But Ryo's work has a way of opening those doors in the mind. After all, if a young woman in Tokyo could see a tsunami fifteen years before it happened, who's to say what else is possible?

Interestingly, the old man never appears in the left-eye dreams — those that look backward into memory or past trauma. He only appears in the right-eye dreams, the ones that peer into the future. That suggests he is tied, not to reflection, but to arrival. He is not there to help us remember. He is there when it's too late to change anything.

Some fear the old man. They see him as death, as the personification of finality. But others view him with compassion. In a world filled with distractions, false alarms, and endless noise, perhaps it is comforting to think there is someone — even just a dream figure — who is truly paying attention. Who sees. Who remembers.

In the quiet mythology of Ryo Tatsuki's dreams, the old man does not demand attention. He does not explain himself. But his presence speaks louder than any prophecy. He stands where the future lands, silent and solemn, bearing witness not to what we fear — but to what we already know, deep down, is coming.

And whether you see him as guardian or ghost, symbol or soul, one truth remains:

He is always there before we are.

The Cracked Earth Vision

Some dreams come with noise — sirens, screaming, rushing water, the thundering collapse of buildings. But Ryo Tatsuki's Cracked Earth vision came in utter silence. It was a still dream, eerie in its calm, as if the world had paused to inhale. There were no crowds running, no weather to speak of. Just a sense that something immense had happened — and that she was arriving only after it was too late.

She first recorded the dream in 1993, though it wouldn't be included in *The Future I Saw* until much later in the complete edition. It wasn't the kind of vision that hinted at a specific date or named a location. There were no landmarks. Only landscape. Earth itself, broken open like pottery. Endless fault lines webbed across flat plains. Great slabs of the ground had shifted and tilted, as if the planet had shrugged its skin. The colors in her sketch were grayscale, as always, but the way she shaded the ground gave it the look of something burned — not by fire, but by pressure. Something beneath had tried to escape.

Ryo stood in the dream, barefoot, in the center of one of these fractures. Around her, entire sections of land were lifted at unnatural angles. Roads stopped midair. Tree roots dangled like veins. There was a river that no longer knew where to flow. It had turned into a still pool between two jagged ridges, reflecting nothing. The sky above was pale, not stormy — the kind of pale that suggested not a beginning, but an aftermath.

She didn't move in the dream. She just looked. She absorbed the overwhelming sense that something irreversible had occurred, and that the world's shape had been redrawn.

When she woke, she immediately began sketching — slowly, more detailed than usual. She wanted to get the cracks just right. Not chaotic, but *measured*. It felt like the damage in the earth had been caused not by nature, but by something deliberate. Something intelligent. She labeled the drawing only with a phrase she wrote carefully along the bottom edge of the paper: *"We didn't listen. Now the ground forgets us."*

This phrase would puzzle her readers for years.

For some, the Cracked Earth dream was an environmental vision — a symbolic reaction to ecological collapse. Deforestation, global warming, the exploitation of resources — all leading to a moment where the earth, quite literally, no longer held us up. Others interpreted the dream as seismic. A warning about a coming megaquake, possibly more severe than the one that devastated Kobe or even the 2011 Tōhoku event. The scale of the damage in her sketch was greater — as if the crust of the earth had come undone in a series of massive ruptures spanning continents.

And then there were those who saw it as metaphorical.

Perhaps, they said, the Cracked Earth dream wasn't about geology at all, but about humanity's collective disconnect — from the planet, from each other, from truth. The dream was a portrait of what happens when our foundations — moral, spiritual, social — begin to collapse beneath us. The ground represented more than physical safety. It was the illusion of stability. And Ryo had drawn what it looks like when that illusion finally gives way.

There's another, more mysterious layer to the Cracked Earth vision: the presence of a strange, geometric object partially buried in one of the deepest fissures. In the sketch, it looks like a cube — smooth, metallic, far too symmetrical to be natural. Ryo never explained it. It's just there, halfway submerged in the earth, as if revealed by the upheaval. She circled it faintly in pencil but didn't elaborate. What was it? Technology? A vault? A remnant of a past civilization? Or something not of this world?

In a note written in the margin of the drawing, Ryo added: *"We weren't meant to see it, but the earth couldn't keep it hidden forever."*

Those few words lit a fire among her more speculative followers. Some believed the cube represented ancient technology — an artifact buried for thousands of years, now exposed. Others connected it to theories of lost civilizations, pole shifts, or even extraterrestrial interference. Whether literal or symbolic, the object added a new, strange dimension to the dream. It suggested that the cracking of the earth wasn't just a disaster — it was a revelation.

What set the Cracked Earth vision apart from many of Ryo's other dreams was its scale. Most of her dreams are centered on cities, disasters, or individuals. But this one felt planetary. Global. It didn't carry the urgency of a warning. It had already happened. It was aftermath, not prediction. And that, perhaps, made it more unsettling than any tsunami or viral outbreak she'd foreseen.

She didn't speak often about this dream. When asked about it by a close friend, she reportedly said, *"That one came from deeper than the others. Not just in the ground, but in time."* What she meant by that is anyone's guess. Was she referring to the dream's connection to prehistory? To the subconscious? Or to something deeper still — a kind of dream that doesn't come from the self at all, but from the collective unconscious, from the earth itself dreaming through her?

Whatever the answer, the Cracked Earth drawing remains one of the most analyzed and debated images in her archive. It holds no date. No names. No narrative. Just fracture. Stillness. Silence. And that haunting phrase — *the ground forgets us.*

It's not a call to panic. It's not even a call to act. It's a moment of recognition. That something is always shifting beneath us. That foundations don't last forever. That the future isn't just what comes next — sometimes, it's what breaks open what we thought could never change.

And when it does, it leaves behind a map. A scar. A dream.

Drawn in pencil by a woman who felt the tremors before the rest of us ever noticed.

The Boiling Sea: A Metaphor?

Of all the recurring images in Ryo Tatsuki's dreams, one of the most disturbing and enigmatic is her vision of the boiling sea. It's not one of her better-known predictions — there's no exact date scribbled in the margins, no obvious geographic setting, and it hasn't (yet) corresponded with any headline-grabbing world event. But it lingers. Maybe because it's so primal. Water — the very element we associate with life, cleansing, peace — turned into a force of slow, simmering destruction. And unlike the tsunami vision, which screamed catastrophe in motion, the boiling sea doesn't roar. It steams.

Ryo described the dream in a brief note dated 1997, written in a tone that was more reflective than alarmed. She wrote, *"The sea looked calm from a distance, but as I stepped closer, it whispered like a kettle. Small bubbles at first. Then foam. Then rising heat. People didn't run — they walked in. They thought it was safe."* That last line is what stuck with her readers. *They thought it was safe.* It shifted the dream from something physical to something symbolic — a warning, maybe, about perception. About slow-burn danger.

In the drawing that accompanied the note, the ocean stretches to the horizon under a blank, low sky. On the shoreline, people gather — but they're not frightened. They stand passively, like beachgoers on an overcast day. Some step into the shallow water. Others kneel to touch the surface. And yet, the closer they get, the more distorted their faces become — not with pain, but with a kind of slack, hypnotic detachment. The only movement in the sea itself is the rising steam. No waves. No wind. Just that slow, eerie hiss.

At first, Ryo didn't include this dream in *The Future I Saw*. It wasn't immediate. It didn't feel like a singular future event. There was no collapse, no disaster point, no emergency to interpret. But years later, when she was asked to revisit her archive for a possible expanded edition, she began thinking about that image again — and whether it meant something more than it first appeared.

Many readers, especially in the post-2011 world, took the boiling sea dream literally. Was it a vision of undersea volcanic activity? An eruption beneath the Pacific? A geothermal event that could send scalding water into the atmosphere? The imagery certainly supported the theory. Ryo had drawn thermal cracks near the coastline, steam vents rising from the deep, and dark birds circling overhead, disoriented. In an age of increasing tectonic awareness and sea-based instability, the idea wasn't entirely implausible.

But other readers — and some of Ryo's closest confidants — believed the boiling sea was not a literal vision, but a metaphor wrapped in dream-logic. A message about society itself. That slow, quiet heating. The illusion of safety. The willingness of people to walk willingly into something deadly because it doesn't *look* dangerous on the surface. What if the boiling sea was about cultural apathy? Or digital addiction? Or environmental denial? The sort of threat that builds in whispers, not sirens.

One interpretation stands out. A journalist who had interviewed several of Ryo's acquaintances after the 2011 disaster once wrote, *"The boiling sea isn't water — it's truth. And we're standing in it, mistaking it for comfort."* It was a haunting idea. That Ryo's dream wasn't about heat or oceans, but about the slow unraveling of collective awareness. The way we accept small changes, small losses, small lies — until the temperature is too high to escape.

In that light, the dream becomes something existential. Not predictive, but diagnostic. It doesn't point to a singular event. It points to a condition. A pattern. One we might already be living in.

What also complicates the dream is the lack of pain in it. The people on the shore don't seem to realize what's happening. They don't scream or suffer. They don't even resist. They dissolve, slowly, into the mist. That's the part that unnerved Ryo most when she talked about the dream years later. *"No one ran. That was the part I couldn't forget,"* she said. There's something deeply disturbing about harm that arrives without resistance — when danger is so well-disguised it feels like comfort.

In subsequent drawings, Ryo hinted that the boiling sea wasn't limited to one dream. It became a recurring backdrop in other visions — a kind of thematic landscape. In a sketch titled *"After the Wave,"* she showed a coastal city completely abandoned. Steam rose in the distance, and the sea glowed faintly. On a wall, graffiti read: *"We warmed it ourselves."* Again, no explanation. Just tone. Just implication.

What gives this dream its lasting power is its ambiguity. It resists analysis. It won't sit still and let us label it. Is it about climate change? Is it a critique of modern passivity? Is it another kind of catastrophe we haven't yet understood — psychological, spiritual, informational?

Or is it, like so many of Ryo's dreams, a mirror?

The boiling sea may not boil with fire, but with consequence. A slow, creeping transformation of the world beneath our feet — and we don't feel it because we've convinced ourselves that the water is just warm. Just cozy. Just familiar.

Until it isn't.

And by then, as Ryo seems to suggest through her quiet pencil lines, it may be too late to get out.

The boiling sea isn't just coming. It may already be here. The question is: are we still standing on the shore... or are we already waist-deep, watching the steam rise, mistaking it for morning fog?

The Mt. Fuji Eruption That Wasn't

Among the many prophetic dreams recorded by Ryo Tatsuki, one of the most debated is the vision of Mt. Fuji erupting — or perhaps more accurately, *almost* erupting. The drawing is striking: Japan's most iconic mountain surrounded by a heavy, unnatural sky, its snow-cap gone, the peak cracked open with dark smoke bleeding upward. The foreground shows travelers abandoning their cars on a highway. Not running. Just walking. Silently. As if the eruption wasn't sudden, but expected.

But here's the catch: Mt. Fuji hasn't erupted.

Not in the waking world, at least. Not yet. And that makes this particular dream an unusual outlier in Ryo's archive — a prediction that still hovers in possibility. A threat held in suspension.

She first sketched the vision in 1991, and her dream notes are brief but evocative. She described hearing a humming sound — not like an earthquake or an explosion, but like a giant engine starting up beneath the earth. In the dream, she wasn't at the mountain, but watching from a distance, through the lens of a camera. Everything felt far away but deeply important. She wrote: *"There was no fire. Only heat. No panic. Just a knowing."* She dated the entry and left it at that, returning only once more to mention it in passing years later, when volcanic activity in Japan began to rise.

What's curious about this vision is that it's less about disaster and more about *anticipation*. The dream doesn't depict Mt. Fuji exploding in cinematic violence. There's no lava consuming towns, no ash choking the sky. Instead, the volcano seems to be *on the verge* — in a state of suspended eruption, like a breath that's never released.

And yet, the drawing is ominous. The cloud above the mountain is too low. The air around it seems warped, distorted. There's a vibration to the image that she managed to capture with her usual sparse, careful line-work. Readers later noted the absence of birds in the sky — a detail Ryo reportedly didn't notice until someone pointed it out. That, too, became symbolic. The silence of nature. The way animals often flee before humans sense what's coming.

The inclusion of this dream in later versions of *The Future I Saw* was met with a mix of fascination and unease. On the one hand, it hadn't happened — and therefore, unlike her visions of the Kobe earthquake or the 2011 tsunami, it couldn't be verified. On the other hand, it hadn't been *disproven* either. It just sat there, on the page, like the mountain itself — massive, ancient, and waiting.

Geologists have long warned that Mt. Fuji is overdue for activity. Its last eruption was in 1707, following a powerful earthquake. Scientists have observed increased seismic movement beneath the region over the years, and contingency plans have been quietly discussed in government and emergency planning circles. The risk is real — but as of now, unrealized.

And that makes Ryo's vision feel eerily present. Like something still pending.

But some readers, especially those familiar with her symbolic approach to dreaming, believe the Mt. Fuji vision was never meant to be taken literally. Instead, they see it as a metaphor — a national reckoning, a pressure point in Japan's cultural psyche. Mt. Fuji isn't just a mountain. It's a symbol. Of balance. Beauty. Stability. To dream of it cracking open is to dream of something deeper being disturbed — the rupture of tradition, the breaking of an illusion.

In this reading, the vision reflects a moment when Japan — or perhaps the world — reaches a breaking point beneath the surface. Not with fire, but with heat. Not with explosions, but with quiet upheaval. The walking travelers in the dream are not escaping a volcano — they are leaving something behind. The old world. The old assumptions. The old sense of safety.

Ryo never clarified which interpretation she believed. She left the sketch unlabelled, as she often did with dreams she wasn't certain of. But she did write something cryptic beneath the image: *"It didn't happen. But the crack is still there."*

That sentence continues to spark discussion. Did she mean the eruption was avoided? Postponed? Or that the danger never existed at all, and the vision was only symbolic from the start?

There's a theory that Ryo's visions don't show fixed futures, but *possible* ones — timelines that might come to pass if nothing changes. In this view, the Mt. Fuji eruption is a dream that never became real because something diverted it. A decision. A shift in human behavior. A collective effort that lessened the pressure.

But there's another, quieter possibility. That it *will* happen — just not yet. That the vision is still counting down, hidden beneath layers of time like magma under stone.

In the years since she drew it, Ryo has not commented further. The mountain stands. The sky holds. And the dream waits.

Whether it was a metaphor, a literal warning, or something in between, the Mt. Fuji vision remains a testament to what makes Ryo Tatsuki's work so enduring. Not just its uncanny accuracy, but its *unresolved tension*. Her dreams live in the space between reality and possibility — like a mountain that hums but does not roar. Like a future that can still be changed.

For now, the eruption remains a dream.

But the crack is still there.

The 15-Year Pattern

By the time scholars, fans, and truth-seekers had sifted through all of Ryo Tatsuki's published and unpublished dream material, a curious question began to rise to the surface: Was there a pattern? Not just in the imagery, or the presence of recurring symbols like the old man or the cracked ground, but in time itself. Were her dreams arriving according to some internal logic or cosmic rhythm?

Eventually, this line of inquiry led to what some now call *The 15-Year Pattern* — a recurring cycle in which major world events she dreamed about seemed to unfold, with startling consistency, roughly every fifteen years. It wasn't a theory that Ryo herself ever wrote about directly, but hints of it are scattered across her dream notes. In the margins, in half-sentences, she sometimes mused on time not as a line, but as something circular, or even tidal. *"It comes back,"* she wrote once. *"Not the same, but again."*

The pattern begins, for most observers, in the early 1980s. That's when her dreams started to carry specific dates and increasingly vivid imagery. In 1982, she dreamt of what we now recognize as the Kobe earthquake. She didn't know it at the time — she only noted the shaking buildings, the panic in the streets, and the newspaper page in the dream with the date: 1995. That's 13 years. Close.

Then came the dream of a massive tsunami — the one where the ocean swallowed streets and rooftops, where she noted the date March 11, with no year. That dream occurred in 1996. The real-world tsunami arrived in 2011. Fifteen years almost to the day.

Then there was the boiling sea, drawn in 1997 — a dream that didn't make much sense at the time. People walking into steaming water, unaware they were in danger. For years it was dismissed as one of her more abstract sketches — until 2020, when the COVID-19 pandemic swept the world in a similarly invisible and deadly wave. The connection wasn't one of direct causality, but of *tone*. A quiet, creeping danger. Slow realization. The same emotional current.

Again, roughly 15 years.

Now, attention has turned to her dream of July 5, 2025 — her most ominous and widely discussed prediction. In that vision, she saw great flooding, a silent sky, and the presence of the old man. There was a sense of something beyond disaster — something cosmically significant, a turning point, not just for Japan, but possibly for the entire planet. The dream was drawn in 2010. Its scheduled echo — if we follow the pattern — is only a breath away.

But the 15-year rhythm isn't only measured in disasters. Some of her softer dreams — ones she never published — also appear to adhere to this cycle. In a dream dated 1984, she drew a woman walking through a field of antennas, hearing voices not from people, but from machines. In 1999, the year *The Future I Saw* was published, a quiet technological revolution was blooming. Global internet access. The rise of digital surveillance. Machine consciousness was no longer science fiction — it was infrastructure.

In another dream dated 2005, she sketched a map without borders, covered in overlapping circles and strange notations in an invented language. She wrote next to it: *"No one owns the sky anymore."* Fast forward to 2020, and the explosion of global satellite constellations — from Elon Musk's Starlink to China's SkyNet — made that metaphorical dream oddly relevant. The sky, once infinite and untouched, was now populated with machinery, watched by systems, monitored by invisible eyes.

It became difficult to ignore. Every 15 years — give or take a year — Ryo's dreams seemed to catch hold of something. Not always the same kind of event. Not always the same level of public attention. But always a *shift*. A bend in the river of time. A moment where reality realigned itself — and Ryo had somehow seen the bend long before the rest of us did.

But how do we explain that?

Skeptics argue it's nothing more than selection bias — that any timeline can be manipulated to match a pattern if you look hard enough. People want meaning. They find it where they can. But those who have followed her work from the beginning, who have read the margins and studied the pacing of her dreams, know it isn't just dates that repeat — it's *feelings*. The emotional climate of her visions. The texture of her dreams. The sense of warning, reflection, and rebirth. Every 15 years, something seems to give way.

Ryo never embraced this theory publicly. She never tried to brand her dreams as a cycle or calendar. But in her later notes, there are more references to recurrence. In a sketch from 2009, she wrote: *"It's like a tide. I can feel it coming in. I don't know what it will bring, but I've been here before."*

The 15-year pattern, if it exists, isn't a prophecy — it's a rhythm. A beat beneath the noise of world events. Ryo was simply one of the few people sensitive enough to feel it and skilled enough to draw it.

And now, with 2025 here, her followers are watching the calendar again. Not out of fear, but out of curiosity. Will the pattern hold? Will the next global moment — whatever it is — once again echo something she dreamed fifteen years ago?

No one knows for sure.

But if Ryo Tatsuki has taught us anything, it's that the future doesn't always arrive with trumpets or thunder. Sometimes, it comes like a tide — slow, subtle, inevitable.

And if you're paying attention, you can feel it before it breaks.

Interpreting the Unfulfilled

Not all of Ryo Tatsuki's dreams have come true. And that, perhaps surprisingly, is one of the most fascinating and vital aspects of her work. For a dreamer so frequently validated by events like the 1995 Kobe earthquake or the 2011 tsunami, it is the *unfulfilled* visions — the strange, vivid, and still-unfolded sketches — that offer the most insight into who Ryo was, and what her dreams might truly mean.

There are dozens of dreams she recorded that remain mysteries. Dreams filled with bizarre symbols, alien landscapes, unfamiliar languages, cities shaped like spirals, entire populations moving underground, and skies filled with objects no one has ever seen in waking life. These dreams didn't come with dates or names. Some didn't even seem to be set on Earth. And yet, they were recorded with the same care, the same urgency, as the ones that eventually matched our reality.

Ryo never treated unfulfilled dreams as failures. She didn't cross them out or dismiss them as mere fantasy. If anything, she seemed to respect them even more. In her private notes, she occasionally referred to them as "quiet dreams," or "ones that haven't found their place yet." She recognized that just because something hadn't happened didn't mean it wouldn't. Or that it even needed to.

A vision not realized could still hold meaning.

There's a sketch from 1992 of a city submerged not in water, but in thick fog. People walk around blindfolded, not because they are forced to, but because they *choose* to. In the dream, Ryo wrote that no one seemed aware of how strange their world was — only that they had all agreed not to question it. She labeled it: *"Vision of Voluntary Blindness."* That dream hasn't come true in any literal sense. But when the world descended into an era of mass misinformation, social media filters, and reality distortions two decades later, readers began to wonder if the fog wasn't weather at all — but a metaphor for the way we choose what to see.

So how do we interpret these dreams that haven't happened? Do we wait for them to unfold? Do we try to decode them, squeeze meaning from symbols, or connect them to emerging news headlines? Or do we let them be what they are — impressions from a dreamer tuned to frequencies the rest of us can't quite hear?

Ryo herself never rushed to decode her unfulfilled visions. She didn't force them into narratives or try to squeeze prophecy out of them. Instead, she approached them with humility. In one note, she wrote: *"Some dreams are only for me. I don't always know which ones until much later."*

This makes her different from self-proclaimed psychics or doomsday forecasters. Ryo never promised accuracy. She never claimed infallibility. Her art was not about prediction as much as it was about observation — even when the thing being observed had not yet arrived. Or may never arrive at all.

Some believe the unfulfilled dreams are glimpses of alternate futures — timelines that *could* have happened if the world had made different choices. If this theory holds any truth, then her drawings are not just about what will happen, but what might have. Futures that now lie discarded, abandoned, avoided, or delayed. If time is fluid — if reality is a branching path — then Ryo may have walked along trails that were never taken, capturing them in her dreams before they vanished from possibility.

Others believe the unfulfilled dreams are metaphysical. Lessons in disguise. Instead of reading them like forecasts, we're meant to read them like mirrors. They reflect not a future event, but a present condition — something we are *feeling* rather than something we are *heading toward*. In this reading, the dreams are internal prophecies. Emotional truths.

A particularly haunting unfulfilled dream, dated 2001, features a crowd standing under a red sky, pointing at a second sun rising beside the real one. There is no panic. Only wonder. Ryo titled it *"False Light."* It has no counterpart in the physical world. But some have interpreted it as commentary on illusion — on our vulnerability to worship the wrong things, to follow lights that only seem real.

And then, there are the dreams that feel *too big* to fit into any one interpretation. One sketch, never included in the original manga but known among her followers, shows a black tower in the middle of the ocean. The ocean has no waves. The tower has no doors. Above it, birds fly in a perfect square formation. Ryo wrote only one word beneath it: *"Patience."*

What are we waiting for? What are the dreams waiting for?

Perhaps the unfulfilled visions are exactly what they appear to be: pieces of a puzzle not yet assembled. Not every dream Ryo had was a postcard from the future. Some may have been warnings we heeded. Some may have been windows we closed. And some — maybe most — were fragments. Not of the future. Not of the past. But of some larger consciousness she brushed against in sleep. A place where symbols mean more than facts, and time folds in ways we can't yet understand.

Interpreting the unfulfilled is not about decoding Ryo's messages. It's about being open to their meaning as it *changes*. A dream that made no sense twenty years ago might feel chillingly relevant today. Or tomorrow. Or never.

The point was never to predict the future perfectly. The point was to remind us that it's already unfolding — and sometimes, if we're quiet enough, we can feel it long before it arrives.

And sometimes, even when it doesn't come, the dream still has something to say.

The July 2025 Catastrophe

Among all of Ryo Tatsuki's visions — the earthquakes, the floods, the masked cities and boiling seas — none has captured the world's attention, anxiety, or imagination quite like her dream of July 2025. It's not just a popular drawing among her readers. It's not just a mystery. It has become a focal point. A looming question mark suspended over the near future. And as the date draws closer, people aren't just reading her manga anymore — they're watching the calendar.

The dream itself is stark and simple, but heavy with emotional weight. Ryo first recorded it in 2010, scribbled hastily into a notebook with a single line underneath: *"July 5, 2025 — 4:18 AM."* That timestamp, precise and unexplained, became one of the most chilling details. Most of her dreams didn't come with exact times. This one did.

In the sketch she made afterward, the image is both quiet and apocalyptic. A street submerged in water. Not from a tsunami wave, but from rising floodwaters that seem to have overtaken the city slowly, steadily. Street signs barely visible. A bicycle half-submerged. What disturbs the viewer most isn't the destruction — it's the stillness. Everything looks abandoned, as if people left not in panic, but in resignation.

And then, in the background, barely more than a silhouette, stands the old man.

There he is again — the enigmatic figure present in many of her future-set dreams. Bearded, still, watching. Always watching. In this dream, he is perched at the edge of a rooftop, gazing over the drowned city. His expression unreadable. Not sorrowful. Not cruel. Just present. As if he knew this was coming. As if this moment had always been inevitable.

Ryo didn't say what city it was. She didn't name a country. But the power lines and street infrastructure in the drawing suggest Japan — possibly somewhere coastal, possibly Tokyo itself. Still, nothing is labeled. She left it as she often did: an impression. A haunting moment drawn with minimalist precision, designed to be felt more than analyzed.

What set this dream apart, and what launched it into international fascination, was the specificity of the date and time. *July 5, 2025. 4:18 AM.* No year range. No ambiguity. Just a line in her notebook that became, for many, a doomsday clock.

As 2025 looms, the internet has exploded with theories. Some believe it predicts a massive natural disaster — perhaps an undersea earthquake between Japan and the Philippines, as a few of her later notes vaguely hinted. Others believe it may involve an unexpected volcanic eruption, even linking it to the long-feared awakening of Mt. Fuji. A few go further, tying it to geopolitical tensions or a global cyber-event — the kind of catastrophe that doesn't destroy cities physically, but plunges them into darkness and silence.

But not everyone sees this vision as a literal prediction. Some interpret the July 2025 dream symbolically — not as a flood of water, but of truth. A metaphor for a great unveiling, a collective reckoning, a moment when people finally *see* what's been rising all along. The old man in the dream, in this interpretation, is not a bystander, but a witness to awakening. He stands not over ruins, but over revelation.

Still others believe the dream is part of her ongoing pattern — the 15-year rhythm. If the Kobe quake hit in 1995, and the tsunami struck in 2011, then 2025 would be the next major turning point. Not necessarily the end of something — but the *beginning* of something else. An irreversible shift. A future Ryo glimpsed long before the rest of us.

In one of her later notes, dated 2011, Ryo quietly revisits the dream. She doesn't add details. She doesn't revise the image. But she writes a single line that many believe is the key to understanding it:

"It wasn't loud. That's what scared me most."

This comment aligns with the tone of the drawing — a world not collapsing in fire or fury, but quietly drowning. Silently transforming. As if the catastrophe is not meant to destroy the world... but to change it.

In that sense, "catastrophe" may be the wrong word. Perhaps what she saw wasn't a disaster in the traditional sense, but a breaking point. A culmination. The moment before the tide turns, when the old world slips beneath the surface and something else — something unnameable — begins to rise.

As the day approaches, it's hard not to feel the tension her dream has created. Some people dismiss it entirely — a coincidence, another prophecy doomed to pass without incident. But others, especially those who've watched her earlier visions come true, find themselves waking a little earlier, watching the skies, and wondering: *what did she see at 4:18 AM?*

No one knows.

But what's certain is that Ryo Tatsuki didn't try to convince anyone. She didn't publish her drawing with warning bells or a dramatic message. She simply drew it. Wrote the date. And moved on.

And now we're the ones standing at the edge of that sketch, watching the water rise. Wondering what it means. Wondering whether it's coming for us — or whether we've already stepped into it.

And whether, somewhere out there, the old man is watching too.

The 4:18 AM Alarm

Among all the unsettling details scattered across Ryo Tatsuki's dream archive, none has stirred as much obsessive speculation as four simple numbers: 4:18 AM. It's written only once — next to the drawing she labeled *July 5, 2025* — and it appears without explanation, squeezed into the margin like an afterthought. But for those who have followed her work closely, that time has taken on an almost mythic quality. It is no longer just a timestamp in a dream. It is a symbol. A riddle. A psychic alarm.

In the dream, as Ryo described it later, she is already awake — not metaphorically, but literally. In her vision, she finds herself sitting upright in a room filled with blue light, as if dawn had arrived but the sun hadn't. There's no noise. No movement. Just that strange, expectant glow. She turns to look at the digital clock beside her bed. It flashes 4:18. She feels, more than hears, something rumble in the distance. But no one else is moving. The city outside her window remains still. Time seems to stretch around her, elastic, suspended.

Then the dream ends.

The drawing that accompanies this note is simple: a flooded street, a collapsed traffic light, and in the background, a building with its top floors glowing faintly — not with fire, but with light that doesn't belong. And high above it all, the old man stands on a rooftop, turned toward the sea. Nothing in the drawing indicates a specific danger. But the feeling is unmistakable: something has just begun. Or maybe just *ended*.

And right there, in pencil, are the numbers: *4:18 AM.*

Why that exact time? Why so precise, when so many of her other visions float freely across time and space?

Some believe it's the moment the event occurs. That something seismic — geological or symbolic — will happen at that precise time on July 5, 2025. Others interpret it less literally. In numerology, the digits 4, 1, and 8 carry meaning. Four is stability, structure. One is origin, the self. Eight is infinity, balance, a turning wheel. Combined, they could symbolize a collapse of order followed by the rise of a new paradigm. Or a cycle completing itself.

Others take a more practical route: perhaps Ryo woke from her dream at 4:18 AM, and the time etched itself into her memory. If so, why include it in the dream drawing? Why not just list the date, as she had done before with March 11 or the year 1995?

Because this dream was different.

Ryo herself offered no interpretation. In her journal, she simply underlined the numbers once. No commentary. But in a note from 2013, she revisits the dream. Not the event, not the water, not the man — just the *time*. She writes, *"Sometimes the body knows before the mind. The time wasn't part of the dream. It was part of me."* That cryptic line has led many to believe that 4:18 AM is more than a moment — it is a *trigger*. An internal signal. An alarm set not by clocks, but by intuition. The hour when the subconscious wakes up first.

There are stories — maybe apocryphal, maybe not — of people waking up suddenly at 4:18 AM over the years without knowing why. Some have claimed to dream of floods. Others of silence. One man in Sapporo reportedly woke from a dream in 2021 in which he was underwater, looking at a blinking sign that read *You're early*. The time? 4:18.

Coincidence? Or something else?

Even skeptics admit that it's an unusual detail to emerge from a dream — especially one with as much weight as Ryo's 2025 vision. If the numbers were arbitrary, why have they embedded themselves into the consciousness of so many? Why do readers return to that exact moment again and again, looking for clues?

Some see 4:18 AM as the "psychic hour" — the time between night and day, when the veil is thinnest. In folklore, this is often when spirits move, when truths whisper, when sleepers shift in bed without knowing why. Ryo may not have been tapping into a date, but into *that space* — the borderland between states of being. The in-between.

There's also the possibility that 4:18 AM marks a window — a symbolic hinge. Not a beginning, not an end, but a threshold. The moment before something crests. The second before a bell rings. In this reading, the time is less about punctuality and more about inevitability. A signal that the event — whatever it is — has *already started*, just beneath our feet.

And yet, perhaps the most compelling interpretation is the simplest: 4:18 AM is the moment the world wakes up. Not physically, but spiritually. A mass awakening. A crack in the illusion. The catastrophe Ryo saw may not be destruction in the traditional sense, but revelation. The moment the tide turns — not outward, but inward.

In that case, 4:18 is not an alarm we sleep through. It is the moment our eyes open.

In a later dream sketch, possibly related, Ryo draws a giant analog clock with no hands, half-submerged in water. In the sky above it, the number "418" is written in cloud vapor, dissolving even as it forms. She labeled the piece: *"You know the time even when you don't look."*

Maybe that's the truth she left for us.

That some things don't need to be explained. Just felt.

And when July 5, 2025 comes, it may not matter what happens *at* 4:18 AM. What matters is whether we're awake when it does.

The Undersea Volcano between Japan and the Philippines

Among the most cryptic and ominous entries in Ryo Tatsuki's lesser-known dream notes is a sketch dated 2009 — a jagged image of a circular ripple radiating from the ocean floor. No coastline. No buildings. No people. Just the deep sea, a rising plume of darkness, and a curious formation of concentric rings suggesting something ancient and volatile stirring beneath the surface. She didn't label it as a volcano at the time. In fact, she barely commented on it at all. But she did add one peculiar sentence: *"It woke up while we were asleep."*

Over time, followers of her work began to revisit this sketch in light of growing seismic activity in the region between Japan and the Philippines — a volatile zone known to be riddled with tectonic tension, undersea trenches, and dormant volcanism. What had once been seen as an abstract drawing now began to resemble something specific, even scientific: an undersea eruption. A deep, slow catastrophe.

This dream never made it into *The Future I Saw*, and yet it has become one of the most discussed in private circles — especially as attention grows around the so-called "July 2025 dream." Some believe this undersea volcano may be *connected* to that event. That it may even be the catalyst.

The region between the Philippine Sea Plate and the Eurasian Plate is among the most active seismic zones on Earth. Volcanologists have long speculated that an undiscovered or slumbering volcano beneath the Philippine Trench could erupt one day — not with lava, but with pressure, steam, and displacement powerful enough to trigger a massive tsunami or atmospheric chain reaction. It wouldn't look like a typical eruption. It would begin silently. With a surge from the deep.

And that is exactly what Ryo's dream looked like.

The sketch shows a vertical column rising from the bottom of the sea — not fiery red, but black and ash-gray, surrounded by circular distortions as if the ocean itself is *trying* to hold it down but cannot. She drew wave lines emanating outward, not tall or aggressive, but *wide* — like invisible shockwaves. In the upper left, a faint scribble that many missed at first: *"Halfway between fire and silence."*

Ryo's description of the dream was vague, but her tone was not. She wrote that she felt *pressure* during the dream — physical pressure in her body, in her ears, in her chest. She woke with a sense of altitude sickness, despite being on the ground. This, to her, was significant. In other dream notes, she always emphasized the *feeling* of a vision — the weight it carried, the emotional residue. This one, she said, felt *ancient*. Like something that had been waiting a very long time.

In speculative circles, this drawing has led to more than one theory. Some believe it foretells a massive undersea eruption that would trigger both tectonic and meteorological disruption across the Pacific — not just a tsunami, but atmospheric interference, disrupting global weather systems. Others believe it's metaphorical: a "pressure event" in the collective psyche, a psychological or societal rupture that begins unseen and only reveals itself once the damage is already done.

But there's a third interpretation — one more esoteric.

A few readers of Ryo's work believe this undersea volcano doesn't belong to our time at all. That the dream is a *memory* rather than a warning — a vision of a cataclysm from a forgotten age. An echo of a past disaster that reshaped the Earth, still lingering in the unconscious ocean of our species. This would place the dream among her "left-eye visions" — the ones that look backward rather than forward.

There is something compelling about this. The drawing lacks urgency. There is no date. No clock. Just a feeling of inevitability, of return. Ryo's only comment about its timing was this: *"It has already begun."*

Some point to more recent seismic activity in the Philippine Sea — rumblings, minor tremors, thermal vent activity recorded by deep-sea probes. These are the scientific breadcrumbs. But Ryo wasn't looking at seismographs. She was dreaming. And in that dream, the sea wasn't angry. It was *tired*. Holding something in. For centuries. Maybe longer.

In the same notebook, several pages after the undersea sketch, Ryo drew a strange figure standing in front of a world map. The continents are cracked. Japan is partially submerged. The man — not the old man this time, but younger — is pointing to the ocean with one hand, and holding a shell to his ear with the other. She labeled the image: *"He hears it before we feel it."*

Who is *he*?

We don't know. But the implication is clear: there is sound beneath the silence. A warning in the deep.

As 2025 approaches, those following her work have begun to watch the region between Japan and the Philippines more closely. Not just for earthquakes. Not just for tsunamis. But for *change* — subtle, creeping, invisible change. Not the kind that happens overnight, but the kind that builds quietly until it cannot be ignored.

If Ryo's dream was literal, the volcano may still be stirring. If symbolic, it may already be erupting in our culture, our minds, our institutions.

Either way, the message is the same:

What lies beneath is rising. Whether we hear it in time... is up to us.

The Mega-Tsunami Warning

Of all Ryo Tatsuki's prophetic dreams, there is perhaps none more viscerally terrifying — and more widely discussed — than the one her followers now refer to as *The Mega-Tsunami Warning*. Though it was not part of the original *The Future I Saw* collection, it has since become infamous through second-hand accounts, private sketches, and cryptic notes discovered in her later journals. Unlike the 2011 tsunami vision, which was eerily accurate and deeply human in its emotional tone, the mega-tsunami dream presents something more mythic — vast, merciless, and beyond comprehension.

The earliest trace of this vision appears in a dream journal dated 2006. The page is water-stained and hurriedly drawn, more chaotic than Ryo's usual calm, minimalist line-work. She sketched a single scene: a city skyline being swallowed by a wall of water so tall it disappears off the top of the page. No detail in the foreground. No people. Just that monstrous wave. The word she wrote across the image — in bold, uncharacteristic ink — was *"unstoppable."*

In a brief note beside it, she added: *"It didn't come from the sea. It was the sea. It rose without warning. No tremor. No time."*

That single line has triggered years of speculation. Ryo had already proven her sensitivity to water-based disasters. Her dream of the 2011 tsunami was so precise — right down to the month — that it silenced sceptics. But this new vision was on a completely different scale. Not a localized disaster. Not a national tragedy. A global one.

She didn't give a date. No city was named. But from the drawing, certain details could be deciphered. The architecture in the foreground resembled a major port city — possibly Tokyo or Osaka, but some believe it looked more like San Francisco, Vancouver, or even Sydney. That uncertainty only deepens the tension surrounding the dream. Was this a vision of a specific place? Or a symbolic portrait of a future every coastal city might one day face?

Years later, in 2014, Ryo returned to this dream. In a different notebook, she drew a variation: the same wave, but this time viewed from far above — from space, it seems. The water is shown sweeping across an entire coastline, moving inland with unstoppable force. On the edge of the wave, she sketched what appears to be a single tower still standing, its top shrouded in birds. The tower is unlabeled. But in the margin, she wrote: *"Some things cannot be escaped. Only climbed."*

Again, no context. No interpretation. Just imagery and feeling.

Some scientists and geologists have looked into the potential real-world parallels. And they are sobering. The threat of a mega-tsunami — one caused not by a typical undersea earthquake, but by a massive landslide, underwater volcano collapse, or asteroid impact — is not fiction. There are known unstable regions along the ocean floor, such as the western flank of La Palma in the Canary Islands, that if dislodged, could trigger waves hundreds of meters tall, racing across oceans in hours. Whole cities could be erased before evacuation was even possible.

But Ryo's dream doesn't point to geology. It points to *suddenness*.

She emphasized over and over that in the dream, there was no warning. No rumble. No animals fleeing. No alarms. Just the appearance of the wave. Fully formed. Already moving.

This, more than anything, unsettles her readers. Ryo's dreams usually carry an atmosphere — a buildup, a foreshadowing. But in this one, there is no "before." Only *after*.

There's a line in her 2016 notebook, written sideways along the edge of a tsunami sketch: *"You won't see it coming because you won't be looking in the right direction."*

Some have taken that to mean the wave will come during a moment of collective distraction — a global event, perhaps, when the world's attention is focused elsewhere. Others think it's symbolic of the human tendency to ignore looming threats until it's too late — climate collapse, unchecked expansion, or our false belief that nature can be tamed.

A few even interpret the wave as psychological. A metaphor for mass collapse — not of infrastructure, but of meaning. A flood of truth, perhaps. One that drowns our illusions.

Yet the physicality of her image — the sheer, overwhelming height of the wave — makes it hard to read purely as metaphor. The way the water moves, the buildings tilt, the windows shatter in waves — all drawn with obsessive detail — suggests that whatever Ryo saw, it felt *real*. Tactile. Cold. Wet. Final.

In her last known note on the dream, from 2017, she writes something simple, and strange: *"It is not a punishment. It is a reset."*

That sentence has become a source of endless debate. If true, it suggests the wave is not malevolent. Not an act of divine wrath or vengeance. But something natural. Necessary. A correction of imbalance. Whether that imbalance is environmental, spiritual, or existential — she never says.

As with all of Ryo's dreams, the Mega-Tsunami Warning is not a prophecy in the theatrical sense. It's not about prediction. It's about presence. A moment suspended in her subconscious that she couldn't ignore. A truth too heavy to speak, so she drew it instead.

And so, the image remains.

A city. A wave. A silence before nothing.

A warning we may not be able to outrun — only *recognize*, if and when it comes. And maybe, just maybe, climb.

The Impact on Japan's Coastline

If Ryo Tatsuki's most ominous visions — from the 2011 tsunami to the unconfirmed July 2025 event — carry any throughline, it's this: Japan's coastline is not a static boundary. It is alive. Shifting. Vulnerable. And in her dreams, it is often the front line of change. For a country defined as much by its relationship to the sea as its ancient temples and futuristic cities, the repeated image of the coast collapsing, drowning, or simply *disappearing* carries both literal and symbolic weight. Ryo seemed to know, long before it became a common theme in scientific reports, that Japan's edges were not secure.

She returned to the shoreline again and again in her sketches. Not always with violence. Sometimes the ocean simply crept forward, swallowing entire roads under a sky that looked indifferent. In one drawing from 1994, she depicted a train track twisted into the water, the steel rails curving like seaweed. No people. Just an empty shoe at the edge of a crumbling platform. In the corner of the page, she wrote: *"It wasn't an event. It was a fading."*

That image feels more relevant now than ever.

In reality, Japan's coastline is slowly shifting due to a combination of tectonic activity, climate change, and rising sea levels. Entire towns are already relocating inland due to coastal erosion and tsunami risk. But in Ryo's dreams, these changes don't happen gradually. They happen suddenly. Without warning. Or they happen so slowly and silently that no one realizes what's been lost until it's too late.

In several of her visions — dated years apart — Ryo draws new shorelines. Not lines of defense, but lines of *retreat*. Land that used to exist is no longer there. In one sketch from 2003, a famous coastal highway is shown submerged, its guardrails sticking out of the water like ribs. Behind it, what remains of a town is blurred, as if melting. She labels the image: *"The map doesn't match the memory."*

This phrase has stuck with many readers. It points to a deeper, more metaphysical fear: not just that the land will vanish, but that *we won't remember what it was.* That the coastline, once a clear marker of identity — physical and cultural — will become a ghost line. A memory overwritten by the sea.

The tsunami of 2011 confirmed many of her earlier shoreline dreams. Entire villages along the Tōhoku coast were wiped away. Some coastlines were physically redrawn. In the wake of that tragedy, officials built massive sea walls to guard against future waves — an act of both engineering and national trauma. Yet in one of Ryo's later dreams, sketched in 2015, she shows those same walls breaking — not from water pressure, but from below. The earth itself rising and shifting beneath them. The title of the sketch: *"The sea was not the enemy."*

Was this symbolic? Was she trying to show that we can't stop change with barriers? Or did she glimpse a literal failure of infrastructure, another disaster waiting to unfold when our defenses — however mighty — meet forces deeper than we can measure?

Even more eerie are the dreams in which the coast changes without violence at all. In one image from 2012, she draws a pier jutting out into nothing. The ocean is gone. What remains is mud, salt flats, and quiet. It isn't the drowning of land she's showing — it's the *retreat* of water. She writes: *"It came and took what it needed. Then left."*

This reversal — the sea pulling back instead of crashing in — adds another layer to the dream landscape. It suggests that change at the coast may not always come with catastrophe. Sometimes it will come in silence. And still, the impact will be irreversible.

It's worth noting that Japan's coastline isn't just geographical. It's emotional. So much of the national psyche is wrapped in its coasts — from the mythic arrival of gods, to the ports of Hiroshima and Nagasaki, to the fishing towns that form the spiritual backbone of the archipelago. When Ryo draws the sea eating the land, she's not just illustrating erosion. She's illustrating identity loss. A shift in how we see ourselves.

And always, in the margins of these drawings, are the small human details. A child's umbrella in the sand. A vending machine half-submerged. A cat perched on a rooftop, waiting for a home that won't come back. These moments remind us that for every meter the ocean takes, there's a human story erased.

Ryo never declared what the final shape of Japan would be. She never drew a definitive future map. But she hinted. In one of her final known sketches — dated simply *"after"* — she draws a jagged, unfamiliar silhouette of Japan, missing its lower curve. Kyushu is gone. Okinawa is just a shadow. The coastline of Honshu is broken like a cracked plate. There are no cities marked. Only light beams rising from where Tokyo and Sendai used to be. She doesn't write a caption. She just draws the sea lapping quietly at the new edge.

And in doing so, she leaves us with the same question again:

Will we wait for the coastline to change?

Or will we finally realize it already has?

Taiwan and Indonesia: In the Path

While much of Ryo Tatsuki's dream-work has focused on Japan and its precarious relationship with the sea, there are scattered drawings and notes — often overlooked — that point southward. Toward Taiwan. Toward Indonesia. Toward nations situated along the trembling Pacific Ring of Fire, where the tectonic plates never rest. These places, in Ryo's fragmented dreamscape, are not just bystanders. They are *in the path*.

In a sketch dated 2007, found in one of her private notebooks rather than her published manga, Ryo drew a sweeping aerial view of a curving island arc. Jagged and smoking. At first glance, it resembles a natural disaster's aftermath — ash clouds drifting, palm trees snapped like matchsticks, shallow waters turned black. In the center, a dot she circled three times: what appears to be Taiwan. The sketch is rough, but it carries her signature tone — haunting stillness.

She didn't write "earthquake." She didn't write "eruption." Instead, she scrawled a phrase in the corner: *"Two islands hold the balance. When one shifts, the other must rise."*

Many believe this cryptic line refers to Taiwan and Indonesia — two nations separated by ocean but bound together by plate tectonics and geopolitics. In recent years, both regions have become hotspots of concern. Taiwan, perched near the converging Eurasian and Philippine Sea Plates, is no stranger to quakes. Indonesia, which spans multiple fault lines, sits atop one of the most volcanically active regions on Earth. These are places used to instability. But Ryo's dream suggests something more than natural unrest. It hints at *timing*. A cause and effect. A shared fate.

In a follow-up drawing from 2010, Ryo sketched two figures on a shoreline, each reaching toward opposite directions. The land between them is cracking. Above, the sky isn't stormy — it's fractured. In a long vertical cloud above the horizon, she wrote: *"The wave comes from underneath, not above. Not because of rain. Because the floor is tired of holding us."* Beneath the image, another line: *"It travels fast — south to north. No time to pray."*

This dream has led to much speculation. Some see it as a vision of a massive undersea quake or a chain of volcanic eruptions that begin somewhere in the Indonesian basin and ripple upward toward Taiwan and, eventually, Japan. Others believe the line *"south to north"* suggests a tsunami triggered near Indonesia that barrels through the South China Sea, affecting multiple nations within hours. If true, Taiwan — with its dense coastal cities and reliance on port infrastructure — would be one of the first in the path.

But there's a deeper question in these drawings: what does "in the path" really mean?

For Ryo, proximity was rarely the full story. Her dreams were as much about *energy* as geography. Taiwan and Indonesia may be in the physical path of rising seas or shifting earth, yes — but they may also be in the *spiritual* path of something larger. A realignment. A rebalancing. In several of her dreams, she referred to "the southern lanterns," an expression she never defined but that many believe pointed to cultures that carry ancient light — wisdom — and are now being tested.

In one sketch, dated 2012, she drew a series of candles floating in water. Some are upright. Some are flickering. Two are nearly extinguished. She labeled them only as *"the watchers,"* and drew a symbol above each that resembled characters from Southeast Asian scripts. She didn't name Taiwan or Indonesia here, but the suggestion is there — that these nations, these cultures, are not just victims of future catastrophe, but *guardians of it*. Bearers of warning.

It's also worth noting that Indonesia has already suffered unimaginable losses from past tsunamis — particularly the 2004 Indian Ocean disaster, which killed over 200,000 people. Ryo was aware of this. In fact, some of her followers believe that event *reset* her dream timeline. That what she saw in earlier dreams as future events may have *partially* manifested already, diverting or delaying the rest.

But the concern remains: what if that was just the beginning?

In her final known notes referencing Indonesia, dated 2016, Ryo wrote: *"The land breaks twice. The first time, we watched. The second time, we forget to look."* That line, chilling in its ambiguity, seems to hint at a second major event — one still ahead. Perhaps even linked to the July 2025 vision. After all, if pressure builds beneath one part of the tectonic plate, it must be released elsewhere. Earth doesn't forget. It remembers.

As for Taiwan, Ryo never depicted direct destruction. But she often drew images of stillness — clocks stopped, boats anchored and unmoving, wires without power. Her Taiwan dreams carried a mood not of sudden catastrophe, but of eerie paralysis. A pause before something begins. Or ends.

So what do we make of these southern visions?

Perhaps they are literal — warnings of undersea eruptions, of earthquakes and tsunamis still to come. Perhaps they are metaphors — symbols of how interconnected our fates are, how one island's shaking is another's silence. Or perhaps they are something stranger still: reminders that what happens in the margins of our world — far from the headlines — may one day become the center.

And if Ryo's sketches are right, the path from Indonesia to Taiwan is not just one of geography.

It is a fuse. Quiet, buried, and almost ready.

The Northern Mariana Islands Threatened

In a quiet, almost forgotten page of Ryo Tatsuki's 2008 dream journal lies a sketch that has only recently been re-examined with a growing sense of urgency. It's not as famous as her drawings of Japan's coastlines or the July 2025 flood. But it may be one of the most quietly foreboding.

The sketch shows a chain of small islands under a dark, roiling sky — the sea churning in slow, spiral-like motion, as if something massive beneath it is about to breach. The islands themselves appear delicate, fragile, barely above the waterline. In the corner, Ryo scribbled a note that reads simply: *"They rise on fire. They do not know they are in the middle."*

At the time, very few linked this sketch to the Northern Mariana Islands. Ryo didn't label them directly. But her drawing style — minimalist coastlines, sparse volcanic peaks, and atmospheric dread — matches the geography of this isolated U.S. territory in the western Pacific Ocean. And the phrase *"in the middle"* now feels eerily literal. The Northern Mariana Islands lie near the deepest trench on Earth — the Mariana Trench — and sit directly along the complex, volatile boundary between the Pacific and Philippine Sea plates.

In her dream notes, she wrote: *"A line beneath the sea cracked like an egg. The water was calm, but the air was loud."* This is a recurring theme in her tectonic dreams — the absence of warning from the ocean itself. No towering wave. No thunderous quake. Just an unseen pressure that releases into the world above in the form of atmospheric disturbance. A sky that *hears* what the sea is about to do.

There is also something surreal in this particular dream. One island in the drawing — likely modeled after Saipan or Pagan — is seen splitting at the center, but not collapsing. Instead, steam pours from the divide, and the vegetation on either side burns without smoke. Ryo drew no people. No infrastructure. Just the land itself, as if it were undergoing a transformation more than a disaster. She labeled the piece *"The Coral Cracked."*

Volcanologists have long regarded the Mariana arc as a volcanic chain of concern. Pagan Island, in particular, is an active stratovolcano, having erupted multiple times in the past century. Nearby Anatahan also erupted violently in the early 2000s. These islands are remote, but geologically alive — with magma chambers, gas vents, and seismic activity beneath their surface. And Ryo — without formal geological training — seemed to sense this.

She returned to this dream in 2011, just months after the Tōhoku tsunami. In a new sketch, she drew the Pacific as if viewed from above — not a flat blue expanse, but a living surface. Beneath the ocean she sketched tendrils of pressure, cracks in red pencil, leading straight to the Northern Mariana arc. Her caption was more assertive this time: *"The hinge begins here."*

What did she mean by that?

Some interpret this to mean that the region could serve as a *starting point* for a larger chain reaction. Not necessarily the epicenter of a single, devastating event — but the *trigger*. A pressure release beneath Pagan or its neighboring islands that sets off a domino effect along the Philippine Sea Plate, through Taiwan, up toward Japan. A whisper that turns into a scream.

If true, this dream may be closely linked with her later sketches of July 2025. It may be the unseen beginning. The moment beneath the sea that awakens the rest of the Pacific. And it may explain why her 2025 vision was so quiet — so *still*. Because the moment had already passed. Far away. Underwater. In a place where few look.

Ryo also hinted at something even more metaphysical. In one of her last known annotations about the region, she wrote: *"The circle does not break at the edge. It breaks at the center."* This sentence has puzzled even her most devoted followers. Is she referring to geography? To energy? To the unseen structures that hold reality together? The Mariana Trench is not just deep. It is mysterious. Myths surround it — about what lies at the bottom, what cannot be measured, what science still does not understand. Ryo may have tapped into that mystery through her dreaming mind.

And still, she did not issue a warning. She never claimed the islands would vanish. Never suggested evacuation. She simply *saw* — and drew.

But the implications are sobering.

If the Northern Mariana Islands are, as she suggested, the "hinge," then we must ask ourselves: what happens when the hinge gives way? When the pressure beneath the most silent part of the Pacific finally finds its voice?

Perhaps nothing.

Or perhaps it will begin everything.

In the world of Ryo Tatsuki's dreams, silence is never peace.

It is the breath before the wave. The crack before the shift.

And the islands?

They wait — small, quiet, listening to the sea.

In the middle.

The Date with Destiny: July 5, 2025

There is something unsettling about writing a future date that already feels mythic. *July 5, 2025.* It sounds like an ordinary Saturday. A midsummer morning in the northern hemisphere. A day when people might plan beach trips, barbecues, or post-holiday vacations. And yet, because of a single pencil stroke in a manga artist's dream journal, that day now looms like an eclipse on the world's timeline — seen by some as coincidence, and by others as destiny.

Ryo Tatsuki never explained why that date came to her. She simply drew it — alongside an image of a flooded city, eerily still, and a solitary rooftop figure watching the aftermath. *4:18 AM,* she noted. No drama. No caption. Just a moment suspended in dream-space. That subtle decision — to not dramatize the vision, to let it speak through silence — made it all the more powerful.

Since then, *July 5, 2025* has been dissected by dream researchers, internet theorists, geologists, mystics, and worried readers alike. It's been discussed on podcasts, examined in spiritual forums, cross-referenced with global seismic records, and even turned into a kind of cultural artifact — a date that now carries with it a strange gravity, even though it has yet to arrive.

So what makes this one date stand out from Ryo's other premonitions?

It's not just the specificity. It's the emotional precision. Most of Ryo's dreams are atmospheric — powerful but open to interpretation. The dream of July 5 is not loud. It's not explosive. It doesn't scream "disaster" in the traditional sense. It whispers. And that whisper is what has captured the imagination of a world increasingly attuned to subtle signals.

The drawing itself is spare: a city partially submerged in water, with street signs barely visible. The waterline is not violent — it's hauntingly still. There are no people visible except for one: the old man. He stands on a rooftop near the horizon, facing away from the viewer, his coat flapping in the wind. He is not running. He is not crying. He is simply *there* — watching the consequence of something that has already unfolded.

Ryo's annotation of the date — *July 5, 2025. 4:18 AM.* — was the only detail she ever gave. But it was enough.

What makes it so compelling is how it contrasts with our usual ideas of catastrophe. We imagine explosions. Alarms. Screaming headlines. But this vision is about *after*. The quiet that follows. The irrevocable change that no one can stop — not because it arrived suddenly, but because it was ignored until it became reality.

And that is what terrifies people most.

Because as we approach that date, it's not just the possibility of a natural disaster that weighs on our minds. It's the feeling that the warning already came — in subtle signs, in overlooked clues, in dreams — and we're still not listening.

Some tie the date to the Pacific "Ring of Fire" — speculating that a chain of seismic events may begin in the ocean trenches, perhaps around Indonesia, the Philippines, or the Marianas, then ripple northward toward Taiwan and Japan. Others believe it has nothing to do with the Earth at all, and instead points to something systemic: a technological failure, a cyber-event, a global shift in consciousness, or a collapse in meaning itself.

There are even those who see it as a kind of spiritual awakening — not destruction, but revelation. The quiet arrival of something long suppressed. A turning point in how we perceive truth, or the beginning of a reckoning for all the things we've refused to face. The dream, in this view, isn't about a wave — it's about clarity. And clarity can be just as disruptive as catastrophe.

Ryo's dream didn't tell us what happens. It showed us what remains after it does.

And the figure of the old man — that eternal observer in her dreams — is the one watching it unfold. Not intervening. Not warning. Watching. Because by the time he appears, it's already too late.

For those who follow Ryo's work, *July 5, 2025* has become a kind of psychic checkpoint. A destination, but also a mirror. We're not just approaching a date — we're approaching a version of ourselves. One that either ignored the signs or finally began to understand them.

Ryo never claimed to predict the future. She never asked to be believed. She drew what she saw in sleep, and let it speak for itself.

Now, that date is nearly here.

The streets may not flood. The sky may not crack. The clocks may not stop at 4:18 AM.

Or they might.

But maybe the most important question isn't what happens on July 5, 2025.

Maybe it's whether, when it comes, we'll be ready to see it — not with fear, but with open eyes.

The Aftermath: Predictions Beyond 2025

If July 5, 2025 marks a pivotal moment in Ryo Tatsuki's dream archive — a quiet catastrophe, a whispered shift, or a subtle ending — then the natural question becomes: what comes next? For most, the story ends with the event. But Ryo never stopped dreaming. Her sketchbooks didn't end at that date. In fact, some of her most curious, cryptic, and haunting visions are those that unfold *after* 2025.

Unlike her pre-2025 dreams, which often focused on isolated disasters or symbolic markers, her post-2025 visions take on a new character. They're less about singular events, and more about the *texture* of the world that follows. A changed climate — not just meteorological, but psychological. Her tone shifts. The drawings become more surreal. The land less familiar. The people fewer.

One dream, dated early 2026, shows a city skyline where the lower half of all buildings has been swallowed by sand. Not water. Not fire. But earth. The roads are intact, but they lead nowhere. On one rooftop, a family eats breakfast as if nothing unusual is happening. The sky is clear. There is no chaos. Only *quiet dislocation*. Ryo wrote beneath the image: *"The world remade itself politely."*

That may be the most unsettling part of her post-2025 visions. There's no longer the violence of quakes or floods. No explosions. No alarms. Instead, there is silence. The sense that a line has been crossed — not with fanfare, but with indifference. As if the world didn't need to collapse. It just *drifted away* from what it once was.

In another dream, dated 2027, Ryo sketches a public square with no people, only screens. Each screen shows a different face, each reciting a wordless message in perfect synchronicity. The sound can't be heard, but Ryo writes: *"They say something that feels like memory, but isn't."* What that means is open to interpretation, but many have linked it to the growing role of artificial intelligence, deepfakes, and simulated reality. Could it be that Ryo sensed a future where reality itself becomes difficult to define?

Then there is the vision from 2028 — perhaps her most conceptually strange. She draws an ocean that no longer moves. Not still, exactly, but *frozen in rhythm*. Waves caught mid-rise, foam suspended in motion. Boats sit on the surface, abandoned, but unmoored. Ryo writes: *"The tide forgot how to return."* Some interpret this as the aftermath of a broken natural cycle. Others see it as a metaphor for human disconnection from nature, or a spiritual stillness that follows a collective trauma.

Another trend in her later dreams is *isolation*. Ryo begins to draw fewer people. Towns appear half-built, or half-forgotten. One sketch simply shows an endless row of apartment buildings with only one lit window. Another shows a street full of open doors — every house abandoned, but orderly. Nothing stolen. Nothing ruined. Just... left behind. She titled it *"The Voluntary Disappearance."*

Perhaps most chilling are the subtle hints that the land itself has changed. A sketch from 2029 depicts a mountain range reshaped into unfamiliar patterns, as though pushed upward by unseen hands. She writes: *"They are not new mountains. They are old ones moved."* What this means isn't clear — perhaps it's seismic, perhaps symbolic. But it reinforces the theme that post-2025 is not about destruction, but transformation.

Ryo also begins to depict the sky more often than the ground. Her dreams start looking upward — not toward celestial awe, but toward something faintly unnatural. Clouds that form perfect grids. Light without source. In one sketch, the stars are missing. The sky is blank. She writes beneath it: *"We turned off the night."*

And yet — for all its mystery and detachment — there are flickers of renewal in her later visions.

A dream from 2030 shows a boy planting something on the roof of a building. Not in a garden, but in a shattered sink. A tiny green sprout. The only color in the drawing. She writes: *"The seeds remembered."* It's one of her few hopeful images. A reminder that life persists — not through strength, but through quiet defiance.

Another dream shows people gathering in silence at a train station where no trains arrive. They don't speak, but they aren't afraid. They sit together on the platform. Some hold hands. Ryo labels it: *"Waiting for something that isn't coming, and finding peace in the wait."*

This tone of acceptance, of stillness, marks the emotional arc of her post-2025 work. It doesn't promise salvation. It doesn't warn of doom. It simply shows a world after the threshold. A world adjusting to new rules. A world that has remembered how to be quiet.

And maybe that's the true message of the dreams beyond 2025.

That after the flood, the cracking earth, the eerie silence at 4:18 AM — the world doesn't end.

It *becomes something else.*

Something not better. Not worse.

Just different.

And if Ryo's dreams are right — we will learn to live in that difference.

Even if we never fully understand it.

The Yokohama Tsunami Vision

Though Ryo Tatsuki never released a formal declaration about it, the vision known among followers as the *Yokohama Tsunami Dream* stands as one of the most geographically specific and emotionally haunting sketches in her entire body of work. It was never widely published. It did not appear in the original printing of *The Future I Saw*, nor in any official compilation of her more recognized dreams. And yet, it continues to circulate in quiet circles — among collectors of her private notes, independent researchers, and those who live with one eye on the coast.

The sketch is undated on the surface, but based on the age of the paper and the surrounding notes, it is widely believed to have been drawn sometime between 2004 and 2006. The drawing shows a city street sloping gently downward toward a harbor. It's unmistakably Yokohama — Japan's second-largest city, and one of its most iconic port landscapes. The presence of the famous Ferris wheel, Cosmo Clock 21, in the background confirms the location. But something is deeply wrong.

In the foreground, Ryo drew water where water shouldn't be. The lower half of the street is submerged. Parked cars are floating at odd angles. The sidewalk is still visible — for now. And in the middle of the water, half-consumed, is a small delivery truck. Its rear doors are open, and its contents — packages, boxes — float outward like debris from a sinking ship.

In the distance, something larger approaches. Not a wave in the Hollywood sense — no towering wall of water crashing dramatically over buildings. Instead, a slow, wide swell moving with unstoppable calm. The sea has risen not to crush, but to *replace*.

The most haunting detail is the woman standing at a pedestrian crosswalk, just above the waterline, holding the hand of a child. They are not running. They are not looking back. They are simply staring straight ahead — toward the water, toward whatever is coming. Their expressions are blank. Not because they are without emotion, but because they have moved beyond it.

Ryo titled the image with only a whisper of ink in the bottom margin: *"The sea stood up."*

This phrase would later appear again, in other sketches, often where silent, creeping water replaced the expected flow of life in coastal cities. But here, in Yokohama, it carries an eerie symbolism. The sea — usually portrayed as something flat, moving, transient — has become *vertical*, present, looming. Not angry, but certain. As if it has decided to assert itself where land once ruled.

In a note written several pages later, Ryo referenced the dream briefly:

"Not a quake. Not a storm. It came from far and low. A pull before a push. Then, all stillness."

This line has given rise to the theory that the vision was not inspired by an earthquake-generated tsunami directly offshore, but by a larger, more distant event — a tectonic rupture or submarine landslide perhaps in the Philippine Trench or Mariana Basin, which sent water toward Japan's coast with little warning and massive reach. This matches the scientific model of "silent tsunamis," where enormous waves can travel across ocean basins without dramatic fanfare, arriving with a deceptive calm — until the water doesn't stop rising.

Why Yokohama?

Of all Japan's cities, Yokohama is unique. It's both densely populated and heavily industrialized, but also scenic, modern, and emotionally symbolic. It represents the blending of Japan's maritime heritage with its global-facing identity. Ryo choosing this city for the setting of such a quiet disaster feels intentional — even if she didn't consciously know why.

The dream has since been connected by some to the larger July 2025 vision, though Ryo never confirmed any date for this particular sketch. Still, its tone matches — not dramatic destruction, but aftermath. Not noise, but resignation. A slow, unopposed transformation. The moment when people stop trying to control nature and simply *witness* it.

In one interpretation, the woman and child represent generations — present and future — both caught in the same inevitability. Not in panic. Not in protest. Just *present*. The sea doesn't roar in this image. It speaks in motion. And they are listening.

What remains fascinating is how different this dream feels from her 2011 tsunami vision. That dream carried fear, chaos, urgency. This one carries inevitability. In fact, in a rare footnote, Ryo wrote:

"There was no fear in the water. Only memory."

That line has puzzled readers for years. Memory of what? A past event? A recurring pattern in Earth's history? A return to something long overdue?

Geologists have since pointed out that Yokohama, while less vulnerable than some rural fishing towns, still sits along low-lying reclamation zones and tightly packed waterfronts that could flood rapidly if a significant tsunami entered Tokyo Bay. A direct hit would be catastrophic, and emergency planning has acknowledged this in recent years. Still, most eyes remain focused on more obvious fault lines. Ryo's dream suggests that may be a mistake.

Not because the risk is greater — but because the stillness hides it.

She saw the water arrive not with fury, but with *purpose*. As if it had a place to be, and a memory to fulfill.

And if she was right, the people of Yokohama — like the woman and child in her sketch — may one day stand not at the edge of disaster, but at the edge of understanding.

Not asking "Why is this happening?"

But simply, *"It's here."*

The 2026 Summer Floods

In the wake of the mysterious July 5, 2025 vision — the dream that captured imaginations and anxieties worldwide — attention has increasingly shifted to what comes next. As we move beyond the psychological and prophetic impact of that single date, some of Ryo Tatsuki's lesser-known but increasingly relevant sketches begin to take on a new urgency. Chief among them is a series of drawings and notes loosely referred to by followers as *The 2026 Summer Floods*.

Unlike her more dramatic, symbolic dreams of earthquakes and waves that reshape entire cities, the 2026 flood sketches are quiet and repetitive. But they are chilling in their cumulative effect. Instead of one large-scale catastrophe, these dreams hint at a season — not a moment — where flood after flood quietly erodes the familiar.

In her notebook dated late 2025, Ryo drew the same location three times over three pages — a narrow river running behind a suburban neighborhood. The first sketch shows the banks full, but calm. In the second, the water has risen to the edges of a playground fence. By the third drawing, the river is gone — replaced by a smooth reflective sheet stretching across rooftops, swingsets, and power poles. There are no people in any of the images. Only shadows in windows. Watching.

Beneath the last image, she wrote: *"Not one flood. Many. The summer did not stop raining. The ground refused to hold it anymore."*

Meteorologists and environmental scientists may find this eerily plausible. Climate data already points to warming oceans driving intense monsoon activity and seasonal rainfall patterns in parts of Asia, Europe, and North America. Urban drainage systems worldwide — including in highly developed cities — are increasingly incapable of handling sustained deluges. The result is not just flash floods, but a *slow saturation*, where concrete landscapes become shallow lakes, and cities begin to sink under their own weight.

Ryo's sketches aren't cinematic. They don't show violent torrents or broken dams. They show water rising slowly in places no one expected: under subway grates, into schoolyards, over highways. In one image from early 2026, she drew a bus shelter partially submerged in knee-high water. A bicycle leans against it, half-underwater. The caption: *"They kept waiting for it to drain."*

There's a tone of denial in these sketches. Not fear, but weariness. A sense that people in her dreams are watching something unfold in slow motion, unwilling or unable to respond. The world is not ending. It's just *changing*, drip by drip.

In a more abstract image — possibly a symbolic piece — Ryo drew a map of a city sliced into puzzle pieces, each floating apart in water. Bridges don't connect anymore. Roads end abruptly. She labeled this one: *"Connections broken by the soft weight of water."* It suggests not only physical isolation, but emotional and infrastructural collapse — the way floods divide communities, interrupt systems, and reveal how little slack we actually have.

Some theorists have tied these dreams to specific regions. One of Ryo's drawings clearly resembles a portion of Osaka's low-lying districts. Another matches the waterfront contours of a European city, possibly Rotterdam or Venice. But many remain anonymous — intentionally generalized. Perhaps because Ryo wasn't trying to show *where* it would happen, but *how it would feel*.

In her notes, she didn't talk about evacuation or disaster response. Instead, she wrote phrases like:

"Children wear boots indoors."

"Mail no longer reaches the other side of town."

"Food grows mold before it reaches the table."

These lines, while poetic, point to real-world consequences — long-term disruptions caused not by one big event, but by the cumulative, creeping damage of constant flooding. In this sense, the Summer Floods of 2026 aren't a spectacle — they're a slow unraveling.

She also alluded to a change in behavior. In a dream dated mid-2026, she drew a line of people climbing onto rooftops not because of a flood, but because the streets had simply become unreliable. She titled the sketch: *"The new ground."* On the back of the page, she wrote: *"Above is safe. Below forgets."*

Ryo's language here becomes increasingly metaphorical — even philosophical. The flooding is not just water. It's a form of memory loss. A washing away of what used to work. What used to connect. What used to make sense. By the time the ground dries — if it ever does — the world it supported may not return the same.

And yet, within all this damp uncertainty, there are hints of resilience.

In one later sketch — likely drawn toward the end of 2026 — Ryo depicts a row of rooftops turned into gardens. The floodwaters remain below, but people above tend to plants, share food, and build makeshift walkways. There are no words on this drawing. Just light pencil strokes and soft lines, as if she, too, was letting the moment breathe.

This is Ryo's post-2025 voice: not panicked, not foreboding — but observant. Quietly certain that the world will continue to turn, but not in the shape we expect. The Summer Floods are not the end. They are the murky middle. A time when systems give way, but life persists — altered, slower, more precarious.

The question isn't whether these floods are coming.

The question is whether we will recognize them when they arrive not with waves, but with puddles that never dry. With skies that forget how to close.

And whether we will choose to wait for the water to leave...

Or learn how to live above it.

The Role of Dreams in Prophecy

As we journey deeper into Ryo Tatsuki's life of visions and drawings, one truth becomes increasingly clear: her dreams were never simply about disasters, dates, or even places. They were about a way of seeing — a relationship between the unconscious mind and time itself. The very idea that dreams could serve as windows into the future, as quiet oracles, as maps written in feeling rather than fact, forms the invisible spine of everything Ryo gave to the world. But to understand her truly, we have to ask a larger question: what *is* the role of dreams in prophecy?

In the modern world, dreams are often dismissed — random firings of the sleeping brain, mental noise, emotional cleanup from the day's events. But for as long as humans have looked up at the stars, dreams have also been sacred. In ancient Egypt, dreams were considered direct messages from the gods. In Greece, oracles often received their visions in sleep. In indigenous cultures around the world, dreaming is still seen as a form of travel — a journey to other dimensions of truth.

Ryo never claimed to be a prophet in the traditional sense. She didn't say, "This will happen." She didn't call herself chosen or divine. What she did was more grounded — and, perhaps because of that, more profound. She *recorded*. She let the dream speak. She gave it shape, through art, and then stepped back. If there was prophecy in her work, it emerged not from prediction, but from honesty. She was not trying to impress anyone. She was trying to understand what she'd seen.

Her process was simple. She would wake, sketch what she remembered, write what she felt, and then move on. No analysis. No agenda. Just the dream, as it was. In doing so, she allowed the dream to remain whole — unedited, untouched by ego or bias. This is where Ryo's quiet brilliance lies: she didn't turn dreams into doctrine. She let them exist as strange artifacts of some other place, suspended between meaning and mystery.

And yet, her accuracy is difficult to ignore.

The Kobe earthquake. The 2011 tsunami. The eerily prescient vision of a masked society before 2020. Dreams she had years, sometimes decades, before those events happened. And not just the content, but the *tone* — the emotional climate of those moments — were captured with haunting precision.

So how is it possible? What mechanism allows a dreamer to see forward into time?

There are many theories. Some believe in a collective unconscious — the idea, made famous by Carl Jung, that beneath the surface of the personal mind is a shared, symbolic language that connects all people and all time. Perhaps Ryo tapped into this deep river. Others suggest she had what some would call precognitive sensitivity — not supernatural, but neurological. An intuitive pattern recognizer, her brain picking up subtle shifts in the world and translating them into dreams long before the rest of us could see the signs.

And then there's the possibility — harder to prove, but strangely compelling — that time itself is not linear. That in dreams, we step outside the straight arrow of cause and effect and briefly glimpse the web-like structure of reality. In that web, a person like Ryo might catch a flash of a future not yet lived — not because she was meant to, but because she was *still enough* to listen.

Ryo often referred to her dreams not as predictions, but as "reflections." She believed dreams didn't tell us what would happen. They reflected what was *already happening* beneath the surface. Our fears. Our path. Our trajectory. She once wrote: *"Dreams don't always warn. Sometimes they remember what we're about to forget."*

And this is where the role of dreams in prophecy becomes clearer. It's not about accuracy. It's about *awareness*. Ryo's visions were never meant to terrify or control. They were meant to *awaken*. To stir something in the viewer — a deeper intuition, a quiet realization, a pause. Not every dream came true. Not every image had a date. But every one invited us to look again. To see what we've missed.

In that sense, Ryo's dreams functioned as emotional barometers. They told us about our relationship with change, with nature, with each other. They weren't just about tsunamis and floods. They were about *how we respond to them*. With panic? With denial? With silence? With resilience?

The prophetic power of dreams lies in their ambiguity. In waking life, we demand certainty. But dreams don't play by those rules. They show us the truth sideways, through metaphor and symbol, through feeling. And sometimes, as Ryo knew, *that* is how the future speaks.

Because the future doesn't always arrive with a bang. Sometimes it comes as a whisper at 4:18 AM. As an image half-drawn in pencil. As a dream that feels too real to forget, but too strange to explain.

And maybe that's why Ryo Tatsuki's legacy endures.

Not because she predicted everything.

But because she reminded us that the future doesn't have to shout to be heard.

Sometimes, it just needs someone to dream it.

Science Meets the Supernatural

The story of Ryo Tatsuki sits at the threshold between two worlds — one rational, empirical, and testable; the other intuitive, symbolic, and inexplicable. Her dreams don't fit neatly into either domain. They exist in a liminal space where science and the supernatural glance sideways at each other, unsure whether to shake hands or walk away. But the longer one studies Ryo's visions — especially the ones that have come to pass with eerie precision — the harder it becomes to dismiss them as coincidence or mere creative intuition. Something deeper is happening here. Something that neither science nor mysticism can fully explain alone.

In many ways, Ryo's life work challenges the long-standing divide between the measurable and the mystical. She wasn't a psychic in the traditional sense. She didn't claim divine insight, and she never monetized her gift. She wasn't even trying to prove anything. She just *dreamed*. And then she *drew*. And then, the world slowly began to line up with what she had seen.

Science, for its part, struggles with this. The scientific method relies on observation, replication, and falsifiability. But precognitive dreams, by their very nature, resist these pillars. You can't predict when a dream will come, whether it will be right, or how to measure the mechanism behind it. Brain imaging can tell us when someone is dreaming, what regions of the brain are active, and perhaps even what types of images they're seeing. But it can't tell us *why* those dreams occasionally seem to reach forward into time.

Yet the discipline of neuroscience doesn't reject dreams entirely. It acknowledges that the dreaming brain is capable of extraordinary pattern recognition — often more creatively and abstractly than when we're awake. Some researchers have suggested that what we call "precognition" may be the subconscious mind assembling data in ways the conscious mind can't, allowing it to "predict" outcomes based on subtle signals we don't know we're absorbing. In that sense, a dream about an earthquake may not be a psychic message — it might be the brain intuitively reading micro-changes in atmosphere, mood, or cultural stress.

But with Ryo Tatsuki, that explanation falls short.

She didn't just dream vague warnings. She dreamed *dates*. *Events*. And she did it repeatedly. She saw the 1995 Kobe earthquake 13 years before it happened. She sketched the 2011 tsunami fifteen years ahead of time. She marked *July 5, 2025* in a dream recorded in 2010 — complete with a time: *4:18 AM*. These aren't abstract themes. They're concrete markers. And they raise an uncomfortable question for science: what if the human mind can do more than we think?

The field of quantum physics, surprisingly, offers some conceptual wiggle room. Theories about time as a non-linear dimension — where past, present, and future exist simultaneously — have found strange resonance in both theoretical science and metaphysical philosophy. Some physicists even suggest that information might move backward through time under certain conditions, or that consciousness might be less local than we assume — not just brain-based, but part of a larger network we barely understand. Could Ryo's dreams be tapping into that web? Could dreaming be a form of temporal perception — not limited by our waking timeline?

Spiritual traditions have long believed this. In Buddhist philosophy, time is cyclical and illusionary. In many indigenous worldviews, dreams are considered sacred — access points to truths not bound by logic or clocks. The shaman dreams not to fantasize, but to retrieve wisdom. The prophet dreams not for self, but for the collective.

Ryo herself never took sides. She never tried to explain the mechanics. She didn't speak the language of scientists, but she also never wrapped herself in mysticism. She simply followed her visions, trusted their timing, and let them exist as they were. If she was a bridge between science and the supernatural, she didn't try to build it. She *was* it — quietly, steadily, without ambition.

In one note from 2014, she wrote:

"It's not about knowing. It's about remembering something that hasn't happened yet."

That sentence captures what so many people feel when they look at her work. A strange familiarity. A moment of recognition — as though Ryo's dreams are not showing us something foreign, but something buried within us. A collective foresight we've forgotten how to access.

Today, scientists are cautiously exploring dream research with more openness. Sleep labs study the predictive functions of the dreaming mind. AI models are being trained to reconstruct dream imagery based on brain scans. But these developments are still far from explaining *why* someone like Ryo Tatsuki could consistently dream things that hadn't happened yet — and be right.

So where does that leave us?

Maybe it's not about choosing between science and the supernatural. Maybe it's about letting them stand side by side, each offering a different lens on the same mystery. Dreams may be neurological processes — and *portals*. Prophecies may be metaphors — and *warnings*. The mind may be a generator of imagination — and *a receiver of signals* beyond time.

Ryo didn't ask us to believe. She only asked us to *pay attention*.

And as we stand now, with July 2025 on the horizon and the world shifting in ways even data can't predict, perhaps her greatest message is that we need both paths — the measurable and the mysterious. The satellite and the dream.

Because maybe, just maybe, the truth is *not* on one side or the other.

Maybe it lives in the space *between*.

Sceptics and Believers

Ryo Tatsuki's quiet life as a manga artist would have remained a curious footnote in the niche world of prophetic storytelling — if not for the accuracy of her dreams. Once a few of her predictions appeared to line up with world events, a fault line opened in public perception. On one side stood the believers, who saw in her drawings proof that time can be touched, that dreams can foretell real disasters. On the other side stood the sceptics, who saw only coincidence, confirmation bias, and an artist's interpretation of fear and fate. And in the middle stood Ryo herself — never claiming, never denying, never explaining. Just drawing.

Scepticism is natural. It's the human mechanism for preserving logic, for keeping chaos at bay. To the skeptical mind, Ryo's work is a pattern-seeking exercise — a case study in how people connect dots where they want to see meaning. The world is full of vague predictions, say the critics. Given enough time, some are bound to appear accurate. They point out that many of her dreams are metaphorical. Open to interpretation. That no scientific mechanism supports the idea of precognition. And that her most famous hits — like the 2011 tsunami — were broad enough that, with a little retrospective framing, they could be seen as fitting almost any large-scale disaster.

But the believers point to the dates. The specificity. The tone. The fact that she drew a world of face masks long before 2020, a tsunami years before it occurred, a cryptic but precisely timed vision of July 5, 2025 — complete with the time 4:18 AM. These weren't predictions offered *after* the fact. They were recorded, drawn, published, and timestamped *years* in advance. For believers, the odds of this being luck or vague metaphor seem slim. They don't see her as a mystic or cult figure. They see her as a receiver — someone unusually tuned to the background hum of something just beyond most people's reach.

This divide has deepened as the world grows more uncertain. With climate disasters increasing, social systems destabilizing, and the very concept of "truth" under siege, people crave meaning. They want signals. They want to know if someone — *anyone* — saw this coming. And for many, Ryo is that someone. Her calm, restrained style never leaned into spectacle. She never profited off fear. That lends her work a kind of moral neutrality. She didn't *try* to be believed. And that made her believable.

Still, the sceptics continue to push back. They point out that we're all vulnerable to confirmation bias — the tendency to remember the hits and forget the misses. They remind us that people predicted the end of the world in 1999, in 2012, in 2020. Nothing definitive happened. They warn that prophecy culture can lead to fatalism or paranoia — that believing too strongly in a predetermined future can prevent us from shaping the present.

But believers argue the opposite: that Ryo's dreams *aren't* deterministic. That they offer insight, not inevitability. Her visions rarely show chaos in real time. They show aftermath. Stillness. The world not destroyed, but transformed. Changed. Her dreams don't scream: *This will happen.* They whisper: *Pay attention.* And in that whisper, many people hear a kind of invitation — to observe more carefully, to listen to intuition, to consider that there might be more happening beneath the surface than logic alone can explain.

Ryo never responded directly to the sceptics. She didn't debate. She didn't defend herself. Her notebooks contain no attacks, no rebuttals, no pleas to be understood. She simply kept dreaming. In one margin, however, she wrote something small and telling:

"They don't have to believe. But they might remember."

That line offers a bridge between the two worlds. Sceptics don't need to accept her visions as prophecy to acknowledge their emotional truth. And believers don't need perfect accuracy to feel the resonance of her drawings. The value of her dreams may not lie in their predictive power, but in the way they make people stop. Reflect. Notice. Prepare.

In the end, the line between sceptic and believer isn't fixed. Some shift from one side to the other after encountering a dream that feels too familiar. Some stay rooted in reason, but admit a quiet wonder. And many simply watch the dates approach — especially July 5, 2025 — with a mix of dread and curiosity.

What unites both camps, however, is this: Ryo's dreams have touched something real. Not provable, perhaps. But real in the way poetry is real. In the way a chill down the spine is real. In the way déjà vu lingers even after logic explains it away.

So whether you believe her dreams are messages from beyond time...

Or whether you believe they're beautifully crafted reflections of human anxiety...

One thing is certain:

You remember them.

The Media's Role in Spreading the Word

Ryo Tatsuki was never a celebrity. She didn't seek interviews. She didn't pitch herself as a seer or brand her drawings as part of any movement. In fact, for many years, her dreams existed in the quietest corners of Japanese manga culture — self-published zines, obscure blog mentions, and handwritten journals shared between friends and readers. But like so many hidden truths, her work was eventually pulled into the spotlight. Not by her own hand, but by a force she never courted: the media.

The role of the media in shaping Ryo Tatsuki's legacy is complicated. It was both a megaphone and a magnifying glass, amplifying her most haunting visions while sometimes distorting the deeper intention behind them. Initially, the press took little interest in her. Her early work was categorized as "dream manga" — a curious niche but not one typically treated with much seriousness. It wasn't until *after* the 2011 Tōhoku earthquake and tsunami that the shift occurred. Her old drawing — a quiet city drowned by water — began circulating online with captions like, *"She predicted it fifteen years ago."*

From there, things escalated. Japanese tabloids began reporting on her with bold, dramatic headlines. TV segments followed, showcasing her earlier drawings in split-screen next to footage of real-world disasters. Her name started appearing in conspiracy theory forums, doomsday blogs, and foreign media outlets looking for "the Japanese Nostradamus." All of this came with very little participation from Ryo herself. She wasn't granting interviews. She wasn't explaining the dreams. She wasn't asking to be believed. And that, paradoxically, made her even more compelling.

Social media platforms accelerated the process. Images of her drawings — particularly the July 5, 2025 vision — began trending years before the date arrived. The mystery of it all became a kind of viral magnet. People who had never heard of her before were suddenly sharing grainy screenshots of her sketches, debating their meanings in comment sections, overlaying them with headlines about global flooding, earthquakes, or rising sea levels. The dream about *4:18 AM* became a meme, a reference point, a kind of online talisman — some sharing it out of belief, others out of fascination or irony.

In this media storm, two things happened. First, Ryo Tatsuki was transformed from a solitary dream artist into a public symbol. Second, her work was pulled in multiple directions at once.

Some outlets portrayed her as a prophet — a woman with mysterious knowledge and a gift for seeing the future. Others framed her as a cautionary tale about the dangers of mass suggestion and confirmation bias. Articles were written both praising her intuitive brilliance and dismissing her as another in a long line of coincidental doomsayers. In between, you had the quiet believers who simply wanted to listen, to reflect, to understand what her dreams were really saying — without spectacle.

The media, for its part, often struggled to navigate the ambiguity of her work. News thrives on certainty — on the who, what, when, and where. But Ryo's visions are built on the *why* — and more importantly, the *what if*. They don't tell a clean story. They suggest possibilities. Emotional truths. Atmospheric warnings. And that doesn't always translate well to headlines.

Still, the attention wasn't entirely unhelpful. In fact, many people only discovered her work because of it. Some began studying dream phenomena, learning about precognition, or becoming more attentive to their own intuitive experiences. Teachers began using her dreams as a gateway to talk about symbolism. Scientists and psychologists found her an intriguing case study. In the whirlwind of media attention, her work — no matter how misunderstood at times — reached far beyond what a self-published manga could have ever done alone.

Interestingly, Ryo never publicly resisted this wave of attention. But she didn't indulge it either. She simply continued sketching in private, never monetizing her notoriety. It was almost as if she knew the media would play its role — that amplification was part of the dream's purpose. Not to warn in the Hollywood sense, but to *stir* something in the collective mind.

And stir it did.

Today, there are entire online communities dedicated to her work — decoding her imagery, comparing past sketches to new events, counting down to dates she once casually recorded in a spiral-bound notebook. Documentaries have been proposed. Books published. News anchors still occasionally invoke her name when disasters strike. Whether they take her seriously or not, they recognize the weight of her presence in the cultural psyche.

But the question remains: did the media help or hurt her message?

The answer may lie in something Ryo once wrote in a margin, perhaps anticipating how her dreams would one day spread far beyond her control.

"The dream reaches only who it needs to. The noise is just wind."

That single sentence reminds us that Ryo didn't dream for headlines. She didn't draw to be believed. She drew because the images came to her. Because the visions wanted to exist.

The media may have spread her work, distorted it, debated it, and dissected it.

But the dream?

The dream remained.

Unshaken. Waiting.

For whoever was ready to see.

The Cult Following of Her Manga

Long before Ryo Tatsuki's dreams began making headlines — before skeptics dissected her timelines or believers shared her sketches across social media — there existed a much quieter, stranger current running beneath the surface: a small but passionate cult following of her manga. These weren't tabloid readers or disaster theorists. They were manga lovers, dreamers, students, artists, night-thinkers. People who stumbled across her early self-published works in dusty Tokyo bookshops or manga conventions and felt, somehow, that they had found a hidden doorway into something otherworldly.

Her manga wasn't flashy. It wasn't commercial. There were no superpowers or love triangles. No climaxes or punchlines. Instead, her panels whispered — sketchy lines, delicate shadows, a mood that lingered after the last page. Each story felt less like fiction and more like an intrusion from another dimension. Some readers described her work as "unsettling in the gentlest way possible." Others said it felt like reading someone else's memory of the future. Nothing was fully explained. Nothing resolved. And that's exactly why it stayed with you.

The early printings of *The Future I Saw* were photocopied and stapled together by hand, with strange dream dates written in the margins. Ryo sold them herself at independent manga fairs, her booth quiet, her gaze modest. She never marketed her work as prophetic. It was dream manga — personal, atmospheric, strange. But some readers noticed something unusual. There was a *pattern*. The drawings weren't just surreal. They were *warning* something.

That's when the cult following began.

At first, it was small — a whisper network of readers who passed her zines around, scanning pages late at night, comparing dates in the drawings to real-world headlines. Forums emerged. Private mailing lists. Fan translations. Readers who had experienced precognitive dreams themselves felt a deep connection to her work. Some claimed her sketches triggered visions of their own. Others simply found comfort in her stillness — the quiet conviction of someone who seemed to see the world differently and didn't apologize for it.

What made Ryo's manga so compelling to this early following was its *tone*. It didn't try to impress you. It wasn't desperate to be believed. There was no manifesto, no worldview to convert to. Just a series of images and fragments — city streets underwater, clocks stuck at strange times, people pausing mid-step as if the sky had just whispered something only they could hear.

And then, the Kobe earthquake struck in 1995.

Readers returned to their copies of Ryo's manga and found a drawing that looked almost identical. The crumbled buildings. The silent city. The date in the margin. Suddenly, what had been a cult fascination became something more.

That was the moment the cult following deepened. Her old zines sold out. People who'd never heard of her began seeking out back issues. Second-hand copies were scanned and passed around online. Some fans began compiling databases of her dreams, categorizing them by type: water, earth, sky, silence. A kind of taxonomy of prophecy.

But even as her audience grew, the *spirit* of her following remained the same — reverent, curious, and strangely personal. For many, Ryo wasn't just a prophet. She was a mirror. Her manga didn't tell you what to believe. It asked what you already *felt* but hadn't put into words. It made people pause. Breathe slower. Listen to the strange currents in their own lives.

Over time, her cult following began producing tribute works — poems, animations, music inspired by her dreams. There were zines inspired by her zines. One group even created a graphic novel based entirely on the idea of "dreams that forget you before you wake," a phrase Ryo once scribbled on the back of a postcard. These works weren't fanfiction — they were spiritual collaborations. A dialogue with a dreamer who never replied, but always seemed to be listening.

When the vision of July 5, 2025 began to circulate, the cult following had already been watching. They knew the drawing. They knew the time — 4:18 AM. They knew the silhouette of the old man standing silently on the rooftop. And while the rest of the world debated its authenticity, turned it into clickbait or fuel for fear, Ryo's followers returned to the drawing with something closer to reverence. Not panic. Not excitement. Just attention.

Today, her work lives in two parallel worlds. One is loud — news stories, Reddit threads, documentaries. The other is quiet — small communities, art exchanges, handwritten letters from people who believe her dreams helped them find peace, or purpose, or a sense that they weren't alone in sensing something deeper under the noise of life.

That quiet world is the one she seemed to draw for.

Her manga wasn't meant to be consumed in a rush. It was meant to be *sat with*. Revisited. Dreamed alongside. It is the kind of art that doesn't demand belief but keeps returning to your thoughts, especially in the still hours before dawn — the same hours Ryo herself seemed to dream most vividly.

Her cult following knows this.

They don't worship her. They don't expect her to be right every time. What they do is something more beautiful — they *listen*.

To the drawings.

To the silences.

To the possibility that sometimes, a dream isn't just a dream.

It's a message left behind... for whoever is awake enough to receive it.

The Auction Frenzy: Collecting Prophecies

It began quietly, the way most things associated with Ryo Tatsuki tend to. A few original pages from *The Future I Saw*, once tucked away in plastic sleeves by careful collectors, began to surface on online auction sites. At first, it was obscure — enthusiasts trading scans, selling photocopies of photocopies, sometimes just passing along grainy JPEGs of hand-labeled dream pages. But then came the tipping point: a drawing from 1996 eerily resembling the 2011 tsunami sold for an eye-watering sum in a late-night bidding war, and suddenly, the market around Ryo's prophetic manga exploded.

What followed was an auction frenzy unlike anything the niche manga world had ever seen. Collectors who once specialized in first editions of Tezuka or rare Shōjo titles were now turning their attention to Ryo Tatsuki's dream pages — not just for their artistic value, but for their potential to *tell the future*.

To some, it was a surreal merging of spiritual obsession and speculative investment. Owning a piece of Ryo's work was no longer about fandom. It was about possession — the belief that her drawings held a kind of residual energy, or even power. There were whispers among collectors that certain sketches "vibrated" differently. That some pages made people dream more vividly after they were brought home. Whether those claims were sincere or just mystique-boosting folklore didn't matter. The legend had taken hold.

What pushed the value even higher was the scarcity. Ryo had never mass-produced her works. Most were distributed in zines with limited runs. Some pages were drawn only once and never scanned. Others were stashed in private journals, kept in boxes under her bed, or gifted quietly to friends. Each surfacing sketch felt like an archaeological discovery. And when one came up for auction — especially with a date, a scene of water, or the figure of the old man — bidders swarmed like storm clouds gathering.

One of the most infamous sales happened in 2022, when a private collector acquired a pencil drawing titled *"The Day the Lights Didn't Come Back"* for the equivalent of $140,000. The drawing, which depicted a flooded subway station with the clock stuck at 4:18 AM, was believed to be linked to the larger July 5, 2025 vision. The bidding war was fierce, involving international buyers from Japan, South Korea, Germany, and a mysterious private client based in Silicon Valley. That purchase confirmed what many had feared — that Ryo's prophecies had entered the high-stakes world of elite collecting.

Soon after, forums began tracking the movement of her pages. Which collector had what. Which drawings had never been digitized. Which pieces were "missing." The most sought-after items weren't even the most detailed — they were the *fragments* with strange captions. Half-dreams. Scribbles. Pages with just a few words and a symbol. These were considered pure, undiluted glimpses into the edge of her unconscious mind. Collectors weren't just buying manga. They were buying *portals*.

And with that obsession came secrecy. Collectors began withholding scans. Some refused to share their finds online. A few even claimed that releasing certain sketches publicly could "distort the timeline." It's difficult to know whether these beliefs were theatrical, spiritual, or just part of the growing mythology around her work. But they added to the mystique — and to the value.

Of course, the frenzy also drew opportunists. Fakes began to circulate. AI-generated sketches mimicking her style appeared on black market sites. Sellers claimed they had "lost dreams" recovered from damaged notebooks. Whole communities emerged online to authenticate her work — parsing handwriting, paper texture, ink aging. Ryo's once quiet and personal dreams had now become the subject of forensic-level scrutiny.

Through it all, Ryo remained silent. She gave no approval. She issued no denials. She didn't comment on the sales, the fakes, or the sky-high prices. Her silence only made her originals more valuable. Every confirmed page with provenance became a kind of sacred object — a fragment of prophecy, art, and mystery all in one.

Today, entire exhibitions are quietly being prepared — curated not by museums, but by private foundations and collectors. One rumored show, tentatively titled *"The Future I Own,"* is said to be assembling over forty original dream pages for a single-night display in Tokyo, timed exactly one month before July 5, 2025. The symbolism is unmistakable. The art world isn't just displaying her work. It's holding its breath beside it.

So what does all this mean?

On the surface, it's just another chapter in the commodification of mystery — prophecy turned into portfolio. But underneath, something more complex is unfolding. People aren't collecting Ryo's dreams because they think they're pretty. They're collecting them because they *believe.* Or at least, they *want* to believe. That the future can be glimpsed. That the past might have warned us. That the answers were always there — sketched in pencil, in a corner of the page, beside a clock stuck at 4:18.

And for some, owning that page feels like owning time itself. Or, at the very least, proof that someone once dreamed the world as it would be — and left behind the evidence.

Folded. Torn. Auctioned. Framed.

But never forgotten.

The Ethics of Predicting Disasters

As Ryo Tatsuki's visions began aligning with real-world events, and her dream sketches found their way into headlines, auctions, and public discourse, a deeper, more uncomfortable question began to surface — one not about accuracy or symbolism, but about *ethics*. What does it mean to predict a disaster? And more importantly, what is the *responsibility* of someone who sees it coming?

For Ryo, these questions were never addressed directly. She didn't speak publicly about morality or duty. She didn't warn governments. She didn't call for evacuation protocols or claim to be a savior. She simply recorded what came to her, dream after dream, and let the world do what it would with those fragments of the future. But as her work grew more widely circulated — especially after the 2011 tsunami, and even more so in the run-up to July 5, 2025 — the weight of those predictions grew heavier.

On the surface, her approach could be seen as passive. But to those who truly studied her, it was clear: Ryo wasn't indifferent. She was *careful*. She knew her drawings had the power to unsettle. She understood the tension between knowing something might happen and not knowing how to stop it. And instead of playing the role of prophet or warning bell, she chose a different path — one that rested quietly in the realm of *suggestion*, not command.

Still, this raises difficult ethical questions.

If someone truly dreams a disaster before it happens — a tsunami, an earthquake, a flood — do they have a moral obligation to warn others? To try to prevent it? To tell someone, *anyone*, who might act on the information?

In the case of Ryo Tatsuki, that wasn't a theoretical dilemma. She had dreams with dates. With places. And they *came true*. Yet she never approached the press with urgency. She never ran to city officials with blueprints of doom. Why?

One theory is that she didn't believe dreams were meant to *change* the future. That they were reflections, not instructions. She once wrote in a margin: *"The dream doesn't ask for action. It asks for awareness."* This idea — that prophecy is not a tool for control, but for consciousness — reframes the ethical debate. Maybe the goal is not to stop the wave, but to prepare the soul.

But not everyone agrees.

Critics argue that withholding specific predictions — especially ones with the potential to save lives — is ethically questionable. If Ryo saw the 2011 tsunami coming, why not speak out louder? If she believed something would happen on July 5, 2025, why not provide more detail? Why not issue a statement, a warning, a plea for preparation?

Believers counter that she did warn — in the only language she had. In pencil lines and date stamps and emotional tone. That her drawings were not *commands*, but *invitations*. Invitations to think differently. To look at the world not just with fear, but with *intuitive attention*. She didn't shout. But she *didn't hide* either.

The ethical challenge is that we don't yet live in a world where dreams are taken seriously. Governments don't mobilize for a vision scribbled in a notebook. Scientists won't act on symbols. Most people forget their own dreams within minutes of waking. Ryo may have understood that to force her visions into the spotlight would not only create hysteria — it would strip them of their meaning. Turn mystery into spectacle.

There's also the issue of *certainty*. Even Ryo, by all accounts, didn't know if her dreams were inevitable. She may have sensed that they were only *possible* futures. Emotional truths, not guaranteed outcomes. To act on them with certainty might have betrayed the very nature of what they were. She didn't want to be seen as a prophet. She wanted to be seen as a *dreamer* — honest, open, unassuming.

And perhaps there's an ethical value in that, too.

In not claiming to own the truth. In not weaponizing fear. In allowing people to come to their own conclusions about what a dream means, rather than telling them how to feel or what to do.

Still, the tension remains. What is the ethical line between art and alarm? At what point does a sketch of rising water become an act of negligence if not shared with the right people? And what happens when a dreamer like Ryo becomes too influential to ignore — when the weight of belief begins to shift from quiet reflection to public expectation?

Some of her followers believe she navigated this line with grace. That her silence was intentional. Protective. Wise. Others feel she held back too much. That more lives could have been saved. That more could have been done.

But Ryo never claimed to be a safety net. Her role wasn't to stop the future. It was to help us *see it* — to sense its outlines, to prepare emotionally for what we might never fully prevent.

Her dreams didn't scream *danger*. They whispered *remember*.

And perhaps that is the most ethical prophecy of all — not to save the world, but to remind us that we're still connected to it. That we are not blind, if we choose to look. That we are not powerless, if we choose to feel.

So in the end, the question isn't just what Ryo Tatsuki *owed* the world.

It's what we owe each other, once we've seen what she saw.

Preparing for the Foreseen

When a dream lingers — not just in the mind of the dreamer, but in the public consciousness — it becomes more than a private vision. It becomes a presence. Ryo Tatsuki's body of work is filled with these presences: floods that don't recede, skies that forget the stars, waves that arrive without sound. The images she left us are not prophecies of fire and brimstone. They are quieter, stranger, more intimate than that. But if even a handful of her visions are more than metaphor — if the floodwaters, the silence at 4:18 AM, the disoriented cities and cracked coastlines are glimpses of what's to come — then one question becomes inescapable:

How do we prepare for the foreseen?

The answer begins, oddly, not with action but with perception. For Ryo, seeing was never just about the eyes. Her sketches, sparse and dreamlike, were less focused on spectacle and more attuned to *awareness*. The people in her drawings rarely run. They pause. They watch. They listen. She seemed to understand that the first step in preparation is *paying attention*. Not just to the external world — to headlines, alerts, newsfeeds — but to the emotional undercurrents beneath it all. To the small shifts in intuition, the sense of timing, the patterns too subtle to make noise but too important to ignore.

In that sense, preparation doesn't start in bunkers or supply kits. It starts in the heart. Ryo's work reminds us that readiness is psychological. It's spiritual. It's the ability to sense when something is ending before it's gone, or to feel when the ground is softening before it breaks.

Still, practical preparation has its place. After all, many of her dreams do involve real-world change. Water rising. Infrastructure failing. Disconnection. Some readers — especially those in coastal regions or earthquake zones — have taken her work as quiet encouragement to build resilience. Not through panic, but through *intentional living*. Knowing your exits. Having backup plans. Living with less dependency on fragile systems. A handful of her most dedicated followers have even moved to higher ground, not out of fear, but from a sense of synchronicity — as if their own dreams confirmed what Ryo had seen.

But she never preached survivalism. Her drawings don't show bunkers. They show rooftops. Gardens on balconies. Strangers sharing food in flooded stairwells. One recurring symbol is a single candle — not in a shrine or a warning beacon, but in a window. A sign that someone is still there. Still alive. Still waiting. Still witnessing.

So much of preparing for the foreseen, in Ryo's world, isn't about avoiding disaster. It's about remaining human inside of it. Preserving memory. Preserving compassion. Preserving the ability to *stay still* when the instinct is to flee — to feel what's happening instead of denying it.

This kind of preparation may seem vague in a world addicted to logistics. We want to-do lists, hard timelines, contingency plans. But Ryo offered something more subtle — a form of inner architecture. She showed us how the world might change *outside*, but also how it might need to change *within*. She seemed to ask: What will you carry when the flood comes? Not what objects, but what beliefs. What memories. What instincts.

In one of her final sketches, believed to have been drawn sometime in 2020, she illustrated a figure walking up a hill carrying only a single item — a chair. At the top of the hill, he sits, facing the sea. Not afraid. Not passive. Just *ready*. The image was titled: *"To witness is to withstand."*

That may be the most distilled version of Ryo's message.

Not to avoid what's coming.

But to be awake for it.

To remain aware in the face of change. To adapt without surrendering the self. To let go of comfort when necessary, but never let go of *presence*. To love more deeply when the world is unsteady. To simplify. To listen. To return to something quieter than panic and louder than denial.

So how do we prepare for the foreseen?

We slow down.

We trust the stillness between events.

We make peace with the truth that some things may not be prevented — but they can be *met* with dignity, with clarity, and with compassion.

We remember that dreams don't always tell us what will happen.

Sometimes they tell us how to *be* when it does.

The Psychological Impact of Prophecies

When a person reads a prophecy — especially one wrapped in eerie precision and poetic silence like those of Ryo Tatsuki — something stirs in the psyche. It's not the same as reading a weather forecast or watching the news. Prophecies touch a deeper part of us. They reach under the rational mind and into that quiet chamber where hope, fear, memory, and myth are stored. And when a prophecy feels real — whether through uncanny accuracy or powerful emotional resonance — it can leave a lasting psychological imprint.

For many, encountering Ryo's dreamwork for the first time is an arresting experience. Her images don't shout. They whisper. And it's that quietness — the way her sketches resist panic and instead evoke stillness — that unsettles people the most. We're used to being startled. We're not used to being *stilled*. Her drawings don't terrify with violence. They disturb with *recognition*. A scene you've never lived but somehow *remember*. A date you've never experienced but can't stop staring at.

Psychologists have long studied the effects of prophecy on human behavior. Prophecy can inspire clarity — a kind of focused urgency — or it can induce helplessness. It depends on the framing. If a prediction is given as an immutable doom, it can trigger paralysis. What's the point of trying if the future is already decided? This is known as prophetic fatalism — a state in which belief in a coming event reduces a person's sense of agency, numbing their willingness to act in the present.

But Ryo's work, paradoxically, often has the opposite effect. It doesn't strip people of control. It invites them to *reclaim it*, not through dominance or prevention, but through emotional presence. Her dream of July 5, 2025, for example, isn't an explosion. It's a moment of still water. The aftermath. The quiet. It suggests something irreversible, yes — but also *acceptance*. It asks: Who will you be when the tide comes? Not can you stop it, but can you *see it*?

That shift — from trying to control the future to learning how to face it — is powerful. And it creates a unique psychological impact: *pre-traumatic growth*. Just as trauma can reshape a person after disaster, the contemplation of an event *before* it happens can also lead to transformation. A deepened appreciation for time. A quiet strengthening of values. A new sense of gratitude. Ryo's followers often report subtle lifestyle changes — less attachment to materialism, more time outdoors, stronger connections with intuition, and, in many cases, more vivid dreaming.

But there's a shadow side, too.

Some individuals fall too far into the rabbit hole. They begin reading every natural event as a sign, every anomaly as a trigger. Anxiety becomes chronic. Dreams become obsessive. A sketch becomes not a mirror, but a trap. This psychological spiral is well-documented in apocalyptic subcultures: the weight of believing you know what's coming can become a burden too heavy to carry, especially when the rest of the world moves on as if nothing is happening.

In this way, Ryo's restraint becomes part of her gift. She never issued commands. She never demanded belief. She didn't tell anyone to prepare bunkers or abandon cities. That refusal to preach — to manipulate with fear — has kept her work from turning cultic. She remained a dreamer, not a messiah. A quiet scribe of images that ask questions instead of enforcing answers.

And this, too, affects the psyche.

Her work teaches a kind of emotional resilience. It asks you to *sit with uncertainty*. To recognize patterns not as fixed outcomes, but as signals. She doesn't scream *run*. She asks *what do you feel* when you see the water rising?

Because the real power of prophecy — psychologically speaking — is not its ability to predict, but its ability to *focus* the mind. To bring attention to the present in a way nothing else can. A compelling prophecy, like a vivid dream, sharpens perception. Colors become more vivid. Moments become more meaningful. You live *as if* the future is watching you, and in doing so, you become more *awake* to your own life.

Ryo's followers often describe a shift after encountering her work. Not panic. Not euphoria. But a quiet internal turning — like a compass clicking into place. They begin to dream more. Feel more. Reflect more. Not just on what *might* happen, but on who they are *now*. In this way, her work acts almost like therapy. Not clinical. Not diagnostic. But spiritual. Symbolic. Soft.

And that may be the most lasting psychological impact of her dreams: not that they change what happens outside, but that they change how we *receive* it inside.

So whether the next great wave comes or not... whether the sky cracks open or simply dims... whether 4:18 AM on July 5, 2025 passes quietly or not at all...

Ryo's visions have already done something profound.

They've made people *look*.

Not just outward.

But inward.

The Global Response to Her Warnings

When the drawings of Ryo Tatsuki began quietly echoing real-world events — from the 1995 Kobe earthquake to the devastating 2011 tsunami, and more recently, the creeping unease surrounding her vision dated July 5, 2025 — the response was anything but uniform. Her warnings, if we even call them that, were not declarations. They were dreams. Fragile pencil sketches. Single sentences in the margin of a page. And yet, they began to ripple far beyond her small audience in Japan. As more of her visions aligned with reality, the global response grew — slow at first, then viral, then fractured.

What makes her case unique is that her warnings did not arrive with sirens. There were no press conferences, no flashing red alerts. Ryo's messages traveled through manga panels and dream journals, through forums, blog posts, art galleries, and whispers. In this way, the response to her work was organic — shaped by culture, psychology, and the personal lens of each person who encountered it.

In Japan, her homeland, the response was both reverent and cautious. Japanese society holds a long, quiet respect for spiritual symbolism and prophetic figures, but also a deep skepticism toward self-proclaimed messiahs. Ryo never claimed the spotlight, and perhaps because of that, she was given a kind of sacred distance. After the 2011 disaster, some in Japan began revisiting her earlier drawings, particularly the one showing a coastal city vanishing under a wave. It was impossible to ignore the parallels. Her books began circulating again. Younger generations discovered her for the first time, while older readers viewed her through a new lens: not as an eccentric dreamer, but as someone who had *seen*.

Elsewhere in Asia, particularly in South Korea, Taiwan, and Indonesia, Ryo's work took on an almost cult status. Her visions were translated, shared in spiritual circles, and even discussed in schools and dream study groups. In nations deeply attuned to both natural disasters and ancestral belief systems, her dreams weren't just seen as warnings — they were *resonant*. A reminder of how fragile and fluid reality truly is. In some communities, Ryo's sketches began appearing on altars, printed and folded into wallets like talismans. Not because people believed every detail would come true — but because they felt that the dream was a message to *listen more carefully to the world around them*.

In Western countries, the response was more polarized. On one hand, journalists and content creators jumped on the mystery. Ryo became a curiosity, a subject of YouTube documentaries, Reddit theories, and TikTok countdowns. Her dream of July 5, 2025, especially with its precise timestamp of 4:18 AM, became a kind of digital myth. Some viewed it with sincere curiosity. Others with skepticism or ironic detachment. A few attempted to "debunk" her work — noting how dream interpretation is naturally ambiguous, or how her drawings can be retrofitted to match real events.

But a smaller, more earnest community in the West emerged — therapists, dream researchers, artists, spiritual seekers — who found in Ryo's work something more than prediction. They saw reflection. Mood. An emotional barometer for the planet. Her followers in these spaces began hosting dream circles, where people would discuss their own visions in light of Ryo's. Her art became a springboard for conversations about intuition, climate grief, and the collective unconscious. She was not just a prophet to them. She was a mapmaker of feeling.

Governments and institutions, predictably, stayed silent.

No agency is going to take official action based on a manga panel drawn decades ago. No emergency system is going to cite "a dream from 1999" as grounds for coastal evacuation. And yet, in quiet corners of certain countries, her visions have been noted. In Japan, some emergency planners privately acknowledge that public curiosity around Ryo's work *has* influenced interest in disaster drills and civil readiness campaigns. In Taiwan and South Korea, some local governments have gently referenced the importance of "listening to all forms of insight" when encouraging awareness of tsunami and seismic risk zones.

But it's the informal response — the one that lives on message boards, in art studios, in late-night conversations between strangers — that defines the true global reaction to Ryo Tatsuki's dreams. Not panic. Not dogma. But *attention*. She has awakened a kind of awareness in people across cultures. A sense that something is moving beneath the surface. That change doesn't always scream. That sometimes it whispers, in pencil strokes and flooded streets no one remembers building.

In 2023, a London-based gallery hosted a small but striking exhibit titled *"Visions of the Possible: Dream as Warning, Dream as Mirror."* At the center was a digital projection of Ryo's most iconic sketches. Visitors didn't just view the art — they *entered* it. Ambient sounds of wind, soft water, and distant alarms played overhead. Notes written by anonymous attendees were pinned to a wall in the final room. One read: *"I don't know if any of this will come true. But I feel like I'm living in the pause before something begins."*

That's what Ryo's work has done around the world. Not convince. Not convert. But remind.

Remind us to pay attention to the atmosphere, not just the forecast. To the tremor beneath the conversation. To the way the future sometimes makes itself known not in events — but in the emotional air around them.

The world has responded to Ryo Tatsuki in many ways: with curiosity, with reverence, with ridicule, with awe. But the most important response — the one she likely hoped for — is still the simplest:

We are watching.

We are listening.

The Intersection of Art and Clairvoyance

In the case of Ryo Tatsuki, the question of whether she was an artist or a clairvoyant has never been easy to answer — because she was both. And the more closely you study her life, her work, and the quietly persistent way her visions have lined up with history, the more you realize that the art and the clairvoyance weren't separate qualities at all. They were part of the same language. For Ryo, the pencil was not just a tool of expression. It was a *receiver* — sketching images not merely from imagination, but from somewhere deeper, stranger, and possibly far ahead of its time.

It's not uncommon for artists to work from instinct. Many describe entering a dreamlike state while creating — what's often called *flow*. But Ryo's version of this went further. Her drawings came from literal dreams, and yet they weren't surreal in the typical sense. They were grounded. Focused. Specific. Buildings, vehicles, signage, dates, times. She didn't interpret these dreams. She *rendered* them. As if she were not dreaming *about* the future, but *visiting* it. And then returning with sketches like a traveler might bring home photographs.

That's where the line between artist and clairvoyant begins to blur.

Historically, visionaries have often used art to express what words could not. Hildegard of Bingen painted her divine visions as intricate mandalas in the 12th century. William Blake merged his spiritual hallucinations with poetry and etchings. The surrealists relied on dreams and the unconscious to access a higher truth. But in all these cases, the art was a byproduct of the experience. With Ryo Tatsuki, the art *was* the experience. It wasn't decoration. It wasn't metaphor. It was *record*.

This is where her work becomes something uniquely powerful — and uniquely difficult to classify. To look at one of her sketches is to witness not just a drawing, but an atmosphere. A moment that has not yet arrived. Her scenes often feel paused, mid-breath. The dreamer has already left. The event has already begun. And we, the viewers, are left to interpret what comes next.

Some critics — and even some believers — have tried to separate the two elements of her identity. They ask: was she a gifted intuitive whose prophecies just happened to be well illustrated? Or was she a brilliant visual storyteller whose symbolic dreamscapes coincidentally aligned with real-world disasters? But to frame it this way is to miss the point. Ryo's drawings weren't prophecy *plus* art. They were prophecy *as* art.

She didn't give interviews. She didn't offer interpretations. She never built a mythology around herself. Her only statement was the page. The sketch. The image. This is where she placed her power — not in persuading us, but in *presenting* something that asked to be felt before it could be understood.

Clairvoyance is often defined as "clear seeing," and that's exactly what Ryo offered — not in terms of analytical clarity, but *emotional* clarity. She saw events not as breaking news, but as emotional temperatures. Her drawing of a submerged street wasn't just about flooding. It was about *resignation*. Her vision of clocks frozen at 4:18 AM wasn't about timekeeping. It was about the quiet horror of *knowing something is wrong and being unable to name it*. These emotional truths were rendered not in statements, but in shadows. In open spaces. In the absence of people.

That absence — the empty streets, the quiet rooftops, the silhouetted figure watching from above — is where her clairvoyance breathes. She knew the viewer would fill in the gaps. That's what art does best: it partners with the subconscious. And that's what clairvoyance does, too. It whispers in symbols, in images, in moments you don't understand until much later. Ryo didn't just tap into that realm. She *translated* it.

And this is why her work has had such a deep and lasting impact.

Not because she was always right.

But because she knew how to *show us what it feels like to glimpse something just beyond reach*. She showed us what the future might look like from the corner of the eye. Not in flashes of lightning — but in a steady pencil line drawn in a quiet room, just after waking.

Today, as her sketches continue to circulate, as we approach the dates she once wrote down without commentary or demand, her legacy doesn't just belong to prophecy. It belongs to *art history*, to *dream studies*, to *spiritual literature*, and to the growing field of psychological aesthetics. Because at the center of it all is one clear truth: Ryo Tatsuki used art not just to reflect the world — but to *see through it*.

And for those who view her work not just as prediction, but as *invitation...*

There lies the intersection of art and clairvoyance.

Not in proving the future.

But in reminding us that we are always — constantly — dreaming it.

The Legacy of Ryo Tatsuki

Ryo Tatsuki never asked to be remembered. She didn't chase attention. She didn't explain her dreams. She didn't market herself as a prophet, a psychic, or a visionary. And yet, decades after her earliest sketches, her name lives on — whispered in forums, studied in art classrooms, debated in newsrooms, and traced with care by believers and skeptics alike. Her legacy is not something built. It's something that *lingers*. Like a dream you can't quite shake.

Her work exists in the margins — literal and figurative. She didn't fill the page with drama. She left space. Space for the dream to breathe. Space for the viewer to enter. Space for the moment between knowing and not knowing to exist without pressure. It's in those margins that her legacy has found its strength. She wasn't loud, and yet she's unforgettable. She didn't predict to alarm, but somehow we still watch the calendar with her dates in our minds.

She wasn't the first to dream of the future. And she won't be the last. But she might be the first who simply showed us what it *felt* like — not in speeches or symbols of divine warning, but in quiet images. A train half-submerged in rising water. A city paused before a wave. A rooftop figure watching, not saving. Waiting, not running. These are the emotions of foreknowledge. Not certainty. Not triumph. But *stillness*.

And in a world that often shouts about the future, Ryo's gift was to whisper it.

Her legacy also lives in the way she blurred the line between intuition and documentation. Between art and archive. Between dreams and data. Her drawings weren't just creative interpretations of unconscious thoughts. They were timestamped, detailed, emotionally coded records of something she *witnessed*. She didn't tell us where her visions came from — only that they came. And then she drew.

And in those drawings, she left behind something astonishing: a body of work that invites us not only to look at the world differently, but to listen to it differently.

Her impact isn't just in the events that appeared to come true. It's in the way people responded — and continue to respond. Artists credit her with teaching them that softness can be prophetic. Psychologists study the psychological effects of precognitive art. Scientists and spiritual thinkers alike now ask deeper questions about how the mind interacts with time. And ordinary people — many of whom had never thought much about dreams — now keep journals, follow patterns, and pay attention to the emotional echoes in their own sleep.

Then there are the growing communities dedicated to protecting and sharing her work. Fans who collect her sketches not for value, but for reverence. Dream circles that trace their beginnings to a single panel from *The Future I Saw*. Curators who now consider her drawings more than manga — seeing them instead as artifacts from an unmeasurable dimension of human experience.

And still, the original vision holds.

That no matter how many people discuss her work, commodify it, criticize it, or canonize it — the dreams were never meant to be loud. They were meant to *linger*. To haunt. To call quietly to the part of you that already knows the future is not a straight road, but a cloud of possibilities. That time may not move the way we think it does. That maybe — just maybe — something in us *already knows*, and dreams are how we remember it.

That is Ryo Tatsuki's true legacy.

Not her most accurate prediction.

Not her most expensive auction sale.

Not even the date July 5, 2025.

But the realization, now shared across the world, that dreams matter. That quiet matters. That to witness is a form of courage. And that sometimes, the most profound messages are given not to save the world — but to help us *see it* more clearly before it changes.

In the end, Ryo didn't want to be believed.

She wanted us to *look*.

And we did. And we are.

Lessons from the Past Predictions

Ryo Tatsuki's dreams were never just about forecasting calamity. They were quiet compositions — soft-edged sketches of moments that seemed too still to matter at first glance. And yet, over time, some of them began to echo real-world events with such eerie clarity that they demanded a second look. It is in that second look — and the third, and fourth — that the real lessons emerge. Not in the shocking precision of a date or a place, but in the emotional patterns that flow through her predictions like an underground river. The question is not just what came true — but what those truths can teach us.

Take the Kobe earthquake, for instance. Her drawing from 1982 showed collapsed buildings and a quiet chaos that mirrored what the world saw in 1995. It wasn't a detailed map or a direct warning. It was a feeling. A still frame of vulnerability. When we look back, the lesson isn't just that she "called it." The lesson is how silently disaster can arrive. How normal everything feels until it doesn't. Her sketch reminds us that fragility doesn't always look like warning signs — it often looks like a typical morning. Until it isn't.

The 2011 tsunami vision offers a different kind of insight. This dream, captured years earlier, carried a sense of inevitability that few could ignore once the wave actually hit. But the lesson isn't found in the rising water or the flooded town — it's in the atmosphere she captured: a world out of breath. People frozen in the face of a force they didn't believe would come. It wasn't just about the sea. It was about our relationship with denial. With scale. With believing that the earth won't remind us how small we are. The lesson is humility. Not fear, but respect.

And then there was the pandemic. Ryo's sketch of people wearing masks in public, drawn in 1995 and filed away like a half-forgotten vision, seemed surreal at the time. But when the world changed in 2020, it was pulled from obscurity and held up as another eerie hit. Still, the real lesson isn't in the masks — it's in how we responded. Her vision shows people standing in place, eyes wide, waiting. Not panicking, just existing in a changed world. It wasn't the disease she captured. It was the *quiet alienation* that came with it. The lesson there is adaptation — the strange ability of humans to get used to anything, even silence, even distance.

Perhaps the most important lesson from all her past predictions is not in what happened — but in how *we* changed in response. Ryo's dreams don't force a conclusion. They show us emotional blueprints. And in studying those blueprints, we're asked to consider how we interpret warning signs. How we prepare for disruption. How we process ambiguity. Because that's what her work is filled with: *ambiguity*. And the more we accept that uncertainty is part of the human experience, the more peace we can find in moving through it.

Another thread weaves through her earlier dreams that's easy to overlook: the value of stillness. Her drawings rarely show the moment of destruction. They show the *breath before*. Or the stillness after. They show people waiting, watching, sitting in the rain, or staring at a line of water rising inch by inch. These moments aren't passive. They're *attentive*. They ask us to slow down. To observe. To get quiet enough inside to *feel* when something has shifted.

If we only see Ryo's past predictions as evidence of her foresight, we miss the deeper teaching. Because a true prophecy isn't just about the event. It's about the *emotional climate* leading up to it. The things we ignore. The routines we rely on. The small cracks we dismiss. What her dreams give us is not a weather report. It's a mirror. One that says: this is how you move through the world before everything changes. And now that you've seen it — what will you do differently?

Even the predictions that didn't come true — or haven't *yet* — still carry value. They aren't failures. They are sketches of potential futures, paths the world might take if it continues in a certain direction. And in that way, they serve as compass points. Not fixed destinations, but warning stars on the horizon.

The lesson here is agency. That just because something has been seen doesn't mean it's locked. Just because a dream feels real doesn't mean it has to be lived. Ryo never insisted that her visions were fated. She seemed to understand that the act of *showing* them might alter their course. That in witnessing, we shift. That in naming the fear, we weaken it.

So what can we learn from the dreams that echoed into reality?

That stillness is powerful. That intuition is not noise. That the future speaks softly before it screams. That preparedness is more than stockpiling — it's emotional readiness. That sometimes the most prophetic act is to *feel deeply*, *see clearly*, and *respond humanely* when the world veers into uncertainty.

And above all, Ryo's legacy through her predictions is this:

A dream is not always a warning. Sometimes, it is an invitation — to wake up.

The Cultural Significance in Japan

To fully understand the impact of Ryo Tatsuki's dreams, one must look not only at the drawings themselves, or at the eerie parallels with real-world events, but at the *soil* from which her visions grew. That soil is Japan — a nation that sits on the boundary between tectonic plates and spiritual dimensions, where tradition and technology coexist, and where dreams are not dismissed as mere fantasy but often treated with quiet reverence. In Japan, prophecy doesn't need to shout. It only needs to resonate. And that is precisely what Ryo's work did.

Her cultural significance in Japan isn't tied to commercial fame or mainstream media recognition. She was never a household name. Her manga didn't top bestseller lists. Her visions didn't appear in prime-time news broadcasts — not at first. Her significance grew more slowly, like a ripple in still water, moving quietly from manga readers to dreamers, from curious students to thoughtful elders, until she became something uniquely Japanese: a *kakureta mono*, a hidden thing of power, known deeply by some and respected from a distance by many.

Japan has always held a particular relationship with dreams. In Shinto belief, kami — spirits or gods — are thought to communicate through natural signs, including visions and dreams. In ancient times, emperors would consult *yume-ura* (dream interpreters) before major decisions. The cultural framework has long allowed for the coexistence of rational governance and spiritual insight. So when Ryo began publishing what she called her "dream drawings," the Japanese public didn't laugh her away. They watched. They listened.

Her early work, seen by many as a form of *mukashi banashi* — old-time storytelling — felt familiar, even when it unsettled. It echoed the tone of old Japanese ghost stories, folk legends, and cautionary tales that didn't so much teach morals as they did instill awareness. Her images weren't warnings in the Western, dramatic sense. They were *omens*. Soft. Inevitable. The kind that don't try to convince you, but quietly follow you into sleep.

When the 1995 Great Hanshin earthquake struck Kobe, a few early readers remembered one of Ryo's sketches — buildings toppled, with soft shadows drawn around them, and a date scribbled faintly nearby. It wasn't enough to prove anything. But it planted a seed. After the 2011 Tōhoku earthquake and tsunami, that seed sprouted. Ryo's drawings began recirculating online and through zines. Her tone, her restraint, her ability to "see without announcing" began to feel... important.

In Japan, this quietness *was* the power. Ryo fit perfectly into the aesthetic tradition of *yūgen* — the profound beauty of the mysterious and the unseen. Where the West might want answers, Japan respected the *not knowing*. And so Ryo's reputation became less about predictive accuracy and more about *emotional truth*. She captured a mood. A forecast of feeling. Her art, while unsettling, never felt manipulative. It felt *respectful* of time, of sorrow, of nature's cycles.

This is also why she wasn't dismissed as a fringe voice. Japan has had its share of cults and false prophets, and the public has grown wary of figures who claim too much. But Ryo claimed nothing. She simply drew what she dreamed. That humility made her culturally trustworthy. Her silence — her refusal to exploit or dramatize her work — allowed people to make their own meaning from it, in line with Japan's respect for personal spiritual interpretation.

The cultural significance of Ryo Tatsuki also lies in how she embodied *mono no aware* — the awareness of the impermanence of all things. Her visions weren't about salvation or doom. They were about *change*. About watching the world shift, knowing you cannot stop it, but also knowing that you can *bear witness* with dignity. That ethos runs deep in Japanese literature, film, and philosophy. Ryo's work was a modern extension of that tradition.

Even today, Ryo's presence lingers in unexpected places. High school students study her drawings in art classes when discussing narrative expression. Dream circles in Kyoto and Fukuoka cite her as inspiration. Psychologists reference her when speaking about trauma anticipation and the Japanese psyche's relationship to nature and inevitability. And among artists, she is often spoken of with a mix of awe and familiarity — the way one might speak of a distant relative who sees things most of us don't.

But perhaps her most enduring cultural role is this: she made dreams matter again.

In an age when logic dominates and data governs, Ryo Tatsuki reminded Japan — and eventually the world — that the dream is still a valid form of knowledge. That it speaks in a language older than words. And that when someone dreams with honesty, humility, and quiet consistency, it is not foolish to listen.

In doing so, she didn't just draw Japan's future.

She became a part of its myth.

The Influence on Modern Manga Artists

Ryo Tatsuki was never mainstream, never part of the high-octane machinery of popular manga culture. She didn't serialize stories in *Shonen Jump*. Her name wasn't shouted from digital billboards in Akihabara. She didn't invent flashy heroes or spin out endless volumes of romantic arcs or battle sagas. Yet her impact on modern manga artists runs deeper than many realize — not through spectacle, but through *subtlety*. Not by loud influence, but by whispering into the creative unconscious of a new generation of storytellers.

The artists who cite her today don't always draw dreams, or even deal with the prophetic. But many are working with the very tools Ryo quietly championed: mood, ambiguity, visual restraint, emotional space. Artists who came of age reading her quiet, foreboding panels in *The Future I Saw* absorbed something different from the action-packed pages they were used to — they encountered atmosphere as a narrative force. They saw that a story doesn't have to shout to matter. That stillness can hold more weight than a scream. And that what's *not* shown often carries more emotional power than what is.

In Tokyo art colleges, aspiring mangaka now study her compositions — how she framed silence, how she used scale to evoke vulnerability, how she rendered isolation with just two lines and a shadow. In critique groups, young artists point to Ryo when asked how to convey emotion without melodrama. Her work has become a kind of template for emotional minimalism. Her influence is there not in imitation, but in instinct — in how modern artists pause the moment before impact, in how they let the reader *feel* something before explaining it.

Several contemporary manga creators have acknowledged Ryo's subtle guidance. Horror artist Shintaro Kago has spoken in interviews about how Ryo's soft visions of dread affected his early sense of timing and unease. Indie creator Yukiko Motoya once said she didn't start sketching in "dream tones" until she came across a photocopied Ryo zine in a friend's bedroom. Manga-ka who dabble in speculative fiction, spiritual realism, or psychological mystery increasingly reference her work as an emotional compass — even if they aren't drawing dreams themselves.

Ryo also opened the door to a new kind of narrative structure — one where cause and effect weren't rigid, and where the reader could live inside the *sensation* of a moment rather than chase a conclusion. In a landscape where many manga still follow linear arcs, character battles, or romantic climax, her influence is most felt in works that live in *suggestion*. Artists influenced by her trust their audience to feel their way through a story rather than be guided point by point.

Visually, her legacy lives on in the way modern artists now embrace *space*. Ryo used white space like another character. Her panels often felt incomplete — not from laziness, but from design. She left gaps for the reader's imagination to fill. Today, many manga artists influenced by her are doing the same. The crowded panels of the '90s are giving way to cleaner layouts, to silence, to pacing that mirrors *breath* more than plot. Some even draw inspiration from her practice of writing dream captions not as exposition, but as poetry — one or two lines of emotional truth that expand the drawing rather than define it.

More symbolically, Ryo's presence has helped validate the idea of the manga artist as *seer*. Not in a mystical sense, but in the way all artists absorb the world and offer it back with clarity. Ryo gave permission to draw without explanation, to say, "This is what I saw," and leave the rest to interpretation. Her reluctance to frame her dreams as truth gave artists a new model of creative honesty. She didn't claim to *know*. She only claimed to *see*.

That humility has deeply influenced artists working outside traditional manga spaces as well — in webcomics, indie visual novels, animated shorts, and hybrid artbooks. There's a growing wave of creators who view manga not just as entertainment, but as *emotional fieldwork*. Many cite Ryo as their silent mentor — the one who made them realize it was okay to show only what they feel. To draw incomplete futures. To trust the dream.

In a 2023 artist residency in Kyoto focused on "Visual Narrative and Intuition," half the participants chose Ryo Tatsuki's work as their primary influence. They didn't draw tsunamis or clocks or masked cities. They drew moments. One artist created a three-panel comic of a child waking up, sensing something outside the window, but never looking. That tension — that restrained intuition — is pure Ryo.

Her legacy continues in the most Ryo way possible: quietly. Through artists who pause more. Who say less. Who draw not because they want to explain the world, but because they feel it shifting beneath their feet. She gave artists permission to tune in, to trust a flicker of a thought, to sketch the thing that doesn't yet have words.

In this way, Ryo Tatsuki didn't just influence manga.

She expanded its language.

The Spiritual Interpretations

Ryo Tatsuki's dreams have been analyzed through every lens imaginable — artistic, psychological, geological, and prophetic — but among the most compelling and enduring responses to her work are the *spiritual* interpretations. These readings do not focus on timelines or disaster forecasts. They do not seek to prove or disprove her ability to see the future. Instead, they ask a deeper question: *What do these dreams mean for the human soul?* And in that asking, a different version of Ryo emerges — not as a prophet of doom, but as a spiritual messenger quietly sketching the metaphysics of a planet in transition.

From the moment she first recorded a vision of buildings swallowed by the sea or streets silenced by unspoken sorrow, something about her dreams struck a deeper chord. Even those unfamiliar with dream work or mysticism often sensed a sacred weight behind her drawings. The empty cities, the clocks stopped at precise hours, the solitary figures watching from rooftops — these weren't just apocalyptic scenes. They were symbols. And like all symbols, they invited reflection. They whispered of *something beyond*.

In Japanese spiritual traditions, especially Shinto and Buddhism, dreams have long been considered a bridge between worlds. The dream realm isn't seen as fake or illusory — it's another dimension of perception, one where spirits, energies, and deeper truths can visit and be visited. In this context, Ryo's work fits seamlessly. She never imposed a spiritual interpretation, but her posture — humble, non-intrusive, open — reflected the sensibility of someone in relationship with unseen forces. She wasn't declaring destiny. She was listening to it.

Many spiritual interpreters have linked Ryo's visions to what is sometimes called *collective karma* — the energetic patterns created by humanity's thoughts, actions, and intentions. In this view, her dreams weren't just personal. They were transmissions from the collective unconscious, or perhaps echoes from a subtle realm of planetary consciousness. The floods, the silences, the crumbling structures — they were metaphors for what we've collectively ignored or suppressed. She was not showing what nature would do to us, but what happens when we drift too far from harmony with nature, with spirit, with each other.

Some believe the old man who appears in many of her sketches — always silent, always watching — is not merely a figure from her dreams but a guide. A kind of spirit guardian, or *bōdhi-sattva*, who appears not to save, but to *witness*. He reflects the spiritual concept of compassionate detachment — holding space without interference, knowing that awakening comes not from being told what to do, but from being shown what is.

Ryo's use of water in her imagery has also invited spiritual symbolism. In almost every major vision, water plays a central role — as a rising force, a mirror, a flood, or a silent sea. Spiritually, water is transformation. It is cleansing. It is memory. In Shinto purification rituals, water is used to prepare the soul for presence. In dreams, it often represents the emotional body, the unconscious, or divine truth. For spiritual readers, Ryo's repeated use of water is not just a warning of physical disaster — it's an invitation to cleanse the self. To face the rising tide within.

Likewise, the times she recorded — 4:18 AM most famously — have been explored in mystical numerology. Four, in many traditions, symbolizes foundation. Stability. The physical world. One is unity. Eight is infinity, cycles, karma. Some readers interpret 4:18 as a moment when the foundation of the world meets its reckoning with the eternal — a cosmic checkpoint, a vibrational alignment, or even a spiritual *call to presence*.

Outside Japan, Ryo's work has found a place among spiritual teachers who explore prophetic art, energy fields, and vibrational shifts in the collective psyche. Her drawings have been used in meditation groups, dream circles, and workshops about global awakening. Not to prepare for disaster — but to become more *receptive*. Ryo's art encourages a turning inward. A softening of certainty. A remembering of something ancient.

One particularly powerful interpretation comes from the idea that her drawings don't predict external events — they reflect *spiritual weather*. The kind that sweeps through culture, emotion, and unseen energetic systems. When she sketches a submerged city, she may be showing us the moment when our collective values are overwhelmed. When a clock freezes, she may be capturing the stillness required before awakening. When people stand silently in rising water, they may be souls choosing — at the deepest level — to meet change with awareness.

This perspective removes the need to "believe" in Ryo Tatsuki as a seer. It invites the reader to see her as a kind of *channel* — one of many who receive glimpses of the world not as it is, but as it *feels beneath the surface*. A seismograph not for earthquakes, but for the soul.

In this way, Ryo's work becomes more than art. More than warning. It becomes *ritual* — a contemplative act. A mirror for the inner world. A tool for awakening. Not by showing what's coming, but by helping us remember who we are when it arrives.

And maybe, in the end, that's the truest spiritual interpretation of her work:

Not prophecy.

But preparation of the *spirit*.

The Role of Intuition in Creativity

In the quiet world of Ryo Tatsuki's dreams, logic rarely leads the way. Her sketches unfold not as planned compositions, but as instinctual transmissions — snapshots of feeling, fragments of time, visual echoes from a place beyond conscious control. And in studying her life's work, one truth emerges clearly: intuition wasn't just a part of her process. It *was* the process. Her entire body of prophecy-infused art was built on the foundation of a single internal compass — intuition. And in doing so, she revealed something profound about the relationship between creativity and the unseen.

Artists have long spoken of intuition as if it were a creative partner — a force that whispers ideas, suggests symbols, leads the hand. But too often in the modern world, intuition is treated as a soft word. Something vague. Untrustworthy. A hunch. Ryo's work challenges that perception. Her drawings aren't careless or impulsive. They are precise, considered, and emotionally weighted. They show us that intuition, when truly listened to, doesn't produce chaos. It produces *clarity* — even when it arrives in the form of mystery.

Ryo didn't create with outlines or scripts. She recorded what she saw in her dreams, as purely as possible, without editing or embellishment. She didn't decode the imagery or attempt to explain it to others. She trusted that the feeling would reach the viewer. This trust — in the vision, in the emotion, in the unknown — is the essence of intuitive creativity. It's not about knowing where a piece is going. It's about *following* the work as it reveals itself.

In one of her rare notes from 1998, Ryo wrote: *"I draw the moment I wake. Before the mind tries to shape it. Before I lose the truth of it."* That moment — the space between dream and interpretation — is where intuition is strongest. It's a fragile place. If you try to understand too quickly, it disappears. But if you trust it, if you let it come through your hand, it becomes something real. Something communicable. Something unforgettable.

Modern creatives, especially those working in visual storytelling, increasingly cite intuition as their creative driver. But Ryo stands out because she never treated it as an accessory. She treated it as a *source*. This allowed her to produce art that feels untethered from trends, markets, or even conscious narrative structure. Her work is rooted not in ideas, but in *atmospheres*. And this is perhaps the highest function of intuition — to access something deeper than logic can hold. To reach into the collective subconscious and return with something true.

What's remarkable is how disciplined her intuition was. Her drawings aren't wild or scattered. They're deliberate. Sparse. Controlled. This shows that intuition doesn't mean lack of form — it means *form that emerges naturally*. When guided by feeling instead of formula, Ryo created images that speak with the quiet authority of dreams. They don't try to impress. They just *are*. And that being — that presence — is what stays with you.

Her process mirrors what many call the "intuitive flow state." A state where the conscious mind steps aside and something deeper — some inner watcher or receiver — takes over. This is where the best creative work often lives. It's not always pretty. It's not always complete. But it *resonates*. It carries a tone, a vibration, a subtle charge that tells the viewer: this is not manufactured. This is remembered.

And what's more, Ryo showed us that intuition in creativity isn't only personal. It can be *communal*. Her dreams weren't just about her. They were about *us*. The fears we share. The landscapes we're moving through. The things we can't yet name but already feel in the atmosphere. By trusting her intuition, she accessed something collective. Something that belongs not just to her sleeping mind, but to the broader emotional field of humanity.

For artists, writers, filmmakers, musicians, and creators of every kind, Ryo's work offers a vital reminder: creativity doesn't begin in the mind. It begins in the body. In the gut. In the subtle twitch of a feeling that says, *draw this, write this, follow this*. You may not know why. You may not know where it leads. But if you trust it, something powerful unfolds.

And in a world increasingly governed by algorithms, data, and engineered trends, intuition is more important than ever. It's the last wild place in the creative landscape — the place where the unknown can still breathe.

So what was Ryo Tatsuki teaching us, beyond the images, the dates, the prophecies?

She was showing us how to listen. How to trust that flicker. How to make art not *about* the future — but *from* it.

And that's the quiet revolution of intuition in creativity:

It reminds us that what's coming often lives within us already.

Waiting. Sketching itself into being.

One dream at a time.

The Debate: Coincidence or Clairvoyance?

As the world inches closer to the dates Ryo Tatsuki once scribbled in the margins of her dream sketches — most famously *July 5, 2025 at 4:18 AM* — the central question surrounding her legacy has grown louder, more urgent, and more divided: *Was she simply in tune with the patterns of life, or was she truly seeing through time?* The debate between coincidence and clairvoyance is not new, but with each global event that seems to echo one of her quiet, ominous drawings, it deepens. It sharpens. And it refuses to resolve.

On one side of the debate are the skeptics — scientists, rationalists, and cultural critics who argue that Ryo's dreams, while haunting, fall well within the boundaries of probability, psychology, and artistic interpretation. They point out that disasters — floods, quakes, pandemics — are not rare. That dreams of destruction, masked figures, crumbling cities, and silence are universal archetypes, not prophetic insights. They argue that what people call "predictions" are really *retrodictions* — interpretations made *after* an event has occurred. That her dreams, while specific-seeming in hindsight, are ambiguous enough to fit multiple outcomes. A wave here. A silent street there. A date that may pass without anything extraordinary. They ask, *Why her?* And, *Why now?*

But the believers — and they are many — offer a different lens. They don't just point to what Ryo drew. They point to *when* she drew it. They reference the Kobe earthquake vision, sketched more than a decade before it happened. The image of a flooded town eerily mirroring the 2011 tsunami. The masked cities she dreamed of years before 2020. And of course, the now-famous July 5th drawing — with its timestamp, its rooftop figure, and its stillness so real it feels like a memory of the future.

For these followers, the question is not *if* she was clairvoyant, but *how*. Some believe she accessed the collective unconscious — a Jungian idea that dreams aren't personal but shared, and that some individuals are more sensitive to what's already taking shape beneath the surface. Others believe she had a rare neurological ability — a hyper-intuition, a brain that picks up on patterns others can't consciously detect. And still others hold a more mystical view: that Ryo was a vessel, a receiver of messages from a realm outside of linear time, chosen not to change the future, but to *show it*.

Ryo herself never entered the debate. She never claimed to be psychic. She never called her drawings predictions. She didn't label her dreams as messages or warnings. She simply recorded them. And in that neutrality, she created space — space for both camps to form, to argue, to interpret, and to return to the images again and again.

But perhaps the question of coincidence versus clairvoyance misses the deeper truth altogether.

Maybe the reason her work matters is not because it tells the future, but because it *reveals* something essential about the present. Her dreams didn't come with explanations. They came with feelings. With atmospheres. With moods we recognize only when the world starts to feel strange again — too quiet, too soft, too close to one of her pencil lines.

Coincidence comforts us. It tells us the world is random, unplanned, and that we remain safely in charge. Clairvoyance challenges that. It suggests we are connected to a web we don't fully understand — a fabric of time and feeling that occasionally slips and lets someone see ahead.

And maybe Ryo was neither lucky nor chosen. Maybe she was just *listening* more closely than the rest of us.

In the end, both sides of the debate return to her images. To the flooded stairwells. The silent rooftops. The woman and child staring at the sea. The old man watching something none of us have seen yet.

The drawing doesn't care who wins the argument.

It waits. Quietly. Patiently.

Just like the future.

And whether we call it coincidence or clairvoyance may not matter as much as we think.

Because Ryo Tatsuki did what very few ever manage:

She made us stop.

She made us *look*.

And she made us wonder — maybe for the first time — if our dreams are trying to tell us something too.

The Future of Prophetic Art

As the world continues to unravel in ways both subtle and spectacular, the work of Ryo Tatsuki stands as more than a singular anomaly — it feels like the beginning of something larger. A shift in how we perceive art, dreams, and time itself. She didn't just sketch moments that resembled the future. She quietly redefined what *art* could be — not just an expression of the self or a reaction to the world, but a *transmission*. And now, the question many are asking, whether consciously or not, is: *what comes next?*

The future of prophetic art doesn't lie in prediction alone. It lies in *attunement*. Artists like Ryo opened a door — one that blurred the boundary between vision and message, between inner truth and outer change. Her legacy hints at a future where creative work is not merely an outlet for emotion or intellect, but a *channel* for perception — one that listens to the world before speaking back to it.

In this unfolding landscape, we are already seeing the seeds of the next wave. Artists are dreaming more. Not just metaphorically, but literally. There are visual storytellers, digital illustrators, and manga creators now citing dreams as central to their process — not as inspiration, but as *source material*. They are beginning to understand what Ryo modeled: that a drawing made in emotional truth, without agenda or ego, can carry *something else*. Something timeless. Something just ahead of now.

Digital platforms have accelerated this trend. Where Ryo's dream zines once circulated hand to hand in quiet corners of Tokyo, today's dream-art is spreading globally through online galleries, AI-assisted storytelling, and even immersive virtual spaces. But with this expanded reach comes a new kind of responsibility. Just as Ryo never exploited her visions or dramatized her insight, tomorrow's prophetic artists must learn to *steward* the unseen rather than *sell* it. There is a thin line between vision and fear-mongering — Ryo never crossed it. And in doing so, she created a model of quiet integrity that future artists would be wise to follow.

As we move further into an era defined by environmental instability, spiritual searching, and technological awakening, the demand for art that feels *true* — not trendy, not commercial, but *resonant* — is only going to grow. People are no longer satisfied with stories that entertain. They want stories that prepare. Stories that comfort. Stories that *warn without wounding*. And prophetic art — like Ryo's — has the capacity to meet that need.

Interestingly, science may catch up in this realm as well. As neuroscience and quantum theory deepen their investigations into consciousness, intuition, and perception across time, the possibility of validating "intuitive vision" may shift from pseudoscience into emerging frontier. The artist, once viewed as a dreamer with no utility beyond beauty, may come to be seen as an essential *sensor* for humanity. A radar for emotional, cultural, even environmental shifts. A pattern-reader. A receiver.

This means the future of prophetic art will not be defined solely by those who *see ahead*, but by those who can *feel into* what is not yet fully formed — those who can sketch a mood before it becomes a headline, who can capture the tension in the air before it breaks into event.

And just as Ryo's dream-sketches were not full narratives but fragments — visual metaphors, glimpses — the prophetic art of tomorrow may shift away from grand, predictive pronouncements and toward *subtle impressions*. The kind that linger. That ask the viewer to look again. To listen differently. To wonder if what they're seeing is not just a scene, but a seed.

New forms will also emerge. Music that carries the memory of what hasn't yet occurred. Films that simulate emotional futures rather than literal ones. Interactive dream archives. Collective dream-mapping platforms. AI models that amplify human intuition rather than override it. In this realm, prophetic art becomes participatory. Not a singular voice telling us what's coming, but a chorus of feeling — a shared subconscious creating a new kind of language, one more responsive than predictive, more poetic than didactic.

And perhaps most important of all, the future of prophetic art will depend on *how we receive it*. Ryo didn't ask for followers. She didn't demand belief. She simply placed her work in the world and let people draw their own conclusions. Her drawings didn't give instructions. They gave *pause*. And in a future increasingly overloaded with noise, that pause — that moment of quiet awareness — may be the most radical offering of all.

So as we look ahead, let us not only ask who the next prophetic artists will be. Let us ask: *Will we listen when they speak softly?* Will we recognize the dream hidden in a single line? Will we allow ourselves to feel what the future *feels like*, not just wait for what it looks like?

Because in that space — that stillness — something is waiting.

And maybe, just maybe...

It's already drawing us.

The Responsibility of the Prophet

The title "prophet" is a heavy one. It suggests wisdom, foresight, and purpose. But it also carries something quieter, more haunting: *burden*. To see what others do not — or cannot — is not just a gift. It is a weight. And in the case of Ryo Tatsuki, who never called herself a prophet but was named one by those who studied her work, the question of responsibility lingers behind every dream, every sketch, every penciled-in date. If you witness something before it happens, what do you *owe* the world?

Ryo never stood on a stage. She never issued proclamations. She didn't use her art to alarm, to manipulate, or to control. And yet, her drawings have been called warnings. Her dream of the tsunami, her eerie vision of masked cities before 2020, and her most discussed piece — the silent rooftop figure in a flooded city on July 5, 2025 — all carry the emotional weight of foresight. Whether they were metaphor or memory of the future, they've stirred people deeply. Which leads us to the core of this chapter: What is the responsibility of someone who sees before others see?

For some, prophecy is a call to action — to shout what's coming, to warn the masses, to try to stop disaster. The biblical prophet, the doomsday seer, the spiritual messenger — they all carry this archetype of the one who *speaks truth to power*. But Ryo never took on that mantle. She didn't stop the clock or plead for prevention. She simply *showed*. And in doing so, she presented an alternative vision of the prophet — one rooted not in authority, but in *humility*.

Her drawings didn't demand belief. They invited reflection. She seemed to understand that timing a future event was not as important as *preparing the soul* to meet it. She didn't seek validation. She allowed her work to be misunderstood, doubted, misread. This restraint, far from being passive, was a kind of deep moral discipline. Because the responsibility of the prophet isn't always to change the future. Sometimes, it's to *record it with grace* — so that when it comes, we are not spiritually unprepared.

Still, the question persists: *Could she have done more?* Some wonder whether she should have spoken louder, pushed harder, sounded the alarm when she saw something terrible approaching. Could more lives have been saved if her 2011 tsunami vision had been delivered to the right person? Could the psychological jolt of July 5, 2025, have been softened if she had explained what she saw?

But these questions, though valid, often miss a crucial truth: Ryo never claimed to know what her dreams meant. She wasn't interpreting. She wasn't forecasting. She was *witnessing*. And perhaps that, in itself, is its own form of service. Because in prophecy, *truth without ego* is rare. And Ryo offered it.

There's also the responsibility of *tone*. Ryo's visions are not panicked. They are not theatrical. They're soft, quiet, emotional. Her drawings don't show chaos, they show aftermath. Still water. Empty streets. The weight of silence. She understood something that many prophets and messengers often forget — that *how* you say something can be just as important as *what* you say. Her responsibility was not to scare. It was to *prepare*.

In many ways, she seemed to be telling us, *you don't need me to warn you*. You already know. You've already seen it in your own way. In your dreams. In your instincts. Her responsibility, then, was not to deliver new information — but to *confirm the feeling already living inside others*. To help people trust their own intuition. To remember what they had forgotten. Her drawings served as mirrors, not commandments.

And then there's the quietest responsibility of all: *to carry the burden with grace*. Ryo bore witness to difficult things. Disasters. Disappearance. Stillness where there should be sound. Clocks that stopped. Futures that broke away from the present. She carried these visions without becoming cynical or bitter. She didn't collapse beneath the weight of them. Nor did she exploit them. She honored the dream by letting it exist without distortion.

That is no small feat.

The true responsibility of the prophet is not to be believed.

It is to remain *honest* to the message, even when it is not understood.

It is to remain *humble* in the face of mystery.

It is to *hold the vision lightly*, knowing the future is not fixed, and yet still showing what was seen — because the *seeing itself* has value.

Ryo Tatsuki fulfilled that responsibility with a kind of sacred minimalism. She didn't speak often, but when she did — through images, captions, or subtle date notations — she spoke from a place of inner clarity.

And that may be the most responsible thing any prophet can do.

To dream truthfully.

To draw carefully.

And to trust that someone, somewhere, will know what to do with what they've seen.

Even if it comes *after*.

The Personal Toll of Seeing the Future

For all the fascination, respect, and speculation that surrounds Ryo Tatsuki's dream sketches, one aspect often gets overlooked — the *cost*. Not to society. Not to culture. But to *her*. Because beneath the mystery of prophetic art, beyond the endless debate of coincidence or clairvoyance, is the simple truth that seeing what may come carries an emotional weight. A psychic exhaustion. A kind of spiritual loneliness that most will never understand. And for Ryo — a quiet woman who never asked to be believed — that toll was perhaps the most private part of her extraordinary gift.

We often romanticize the idea of the visionary — the dreamer who glimpses the future and steps forward as a guide. But rarely do we speak of the isolation that comes with that role. To see something before others do is to live out of sync with the present. To exist in the tension between now and not-yet. Ryo did not receive her visions with joy or pride. She *recorded* them. As if they were burdens, not insights. She woke in the early hours of the morning — sometimes terrified, sometimes numb — and instead of dismissing the images, she drew them. Quietly. Dutifully. Alone.

She didn't tell the world what to do. She didn't argue for her dreams to be seen as truth. That restraint, so admired by those who study her work now, came at a cost. Because when you see disaster in a dream — cities under water, buildings cracked open, people in masks, dates circled in the future — and you have *no idea* what it means or what to do with it, you are not empowered. You are *haunted*.

There's a loneliness in knowing too much — or believing you might — and having no language to communicate it. Ryo wasn't a scientist. She wasn't a priest. She was an artist with a pencil and a recurring sense that something was approaching. How does a person live with that? How do you return to ordinary life, to morning routines and polite conversation, when part of your mind is still on a rooftop watching the sea rise?

Ryo's notebooks reveal signs of this toll. Not in melodrama, but in tone. Her notes became shorter over time. Her captions more cryptic. Her figures more isolated. Often, her dreamscapes feature no one at all — just the world, altered. Changed. Abandoned. It's as though the more she saw, the less she felt able to explain. Or perhaps the more she accepted that these visions were hers to carry, but not to fix.

She never tried to monetize her work. Never gave in to the allure of the spotlight. But that didn't mean she was unaffected by attention. As her drawings resurfaced around the time of the 2011 tsunami and again during the COVID-19 pandemic, she became aware that people were looking to her — wanting answers, warnings, clarity. But Ryo had none of those things. Only *images*. And it's not hard to imagine how overwhelming that pressure must have felt.

To see the future is not just to witness external change. It's to feel time differently. To feel *disconnected* from the present — like you're living in anticipation of something others don't yet sense. This disconnect can erode the psyche. It creates a subtle distance between the seer and the seen. Between the prophet and the world she lives in.

Ryo once wrote in the corner of a dream page: *"The moment I draw it, I feel further from people."* That sentence — so simple, so quiet — reveals the deeper ache beneath her gift. The human cost of being the one who watches.

And yet, she never stopped drawing.

Perhaps she found relief in the act of creation. Perhaps the page was the only place where the weight of her visions could rest. Where she could lay down what she'd seen without judgment, without the burden of interpretation, without fear of disbelief. In that sense, drawing wasn't just her method. It was her therapy. Her ritual. Her silent conversation with something larger than herself.

But the emotional toll doesn't disappear just because it's recorded. Dreams like hers don't fade like ordinary dreams. They return. They repeat. And Ryo was caught in that rhythm — waking, seeing, drawing, waiting. Sometimes for years. Sometimes for decades. Never knowing what would come of what she saw.

There's also the fear — not just of being disbelieved, but of being *right*. How does a person live with the knowledge that something terrible might unfold exactly as they dreamed it? That a flooded street or a cracked cityscape or a date and time might come true?

For some, that fear turns to panic. For others, denial. But Ryo seemed to live in quiet surrender — not to the events, but to the role she never asked for.

And this is the final toll: *identity*. To be called a prophet when you only ever saw yourself as a dreamer is to lose a part of who you were. Ryo did not seek the title. She never publicly accepted it. But once the world began seeing her that way, it must have been hard to just *be* Ryo again — an artist. A woman. A person. Not a symbol.

She bore it with grace. But make no mistake — she *bore* it.

And in that burden, there is a kind of quiet heroism.

Because it reminds us that seeing the future isn't glamorous.

It's heavy. It's lonely. It's exhausting.

But in Ryo Tatsuki's case, it was also *deeply human*.

She didn't predict the future to impress us.

She dreamed it because she couldn't help but see. And then she drew because she couldn't bear to forget.

And maybe, in doing so, she made the burden a little lighter — not just for herself, but for anyone who has ever dreamed something before the world was ready.

The Line between Dream and Reality

For most people, dreams are a private chaos — fleeting flashes of nonsense, abstract longings, fears stitched together with the day's residue and the mind's wandering. We wake, we forget, and we move on. But for Ryo Tatsuki, that line between dream and reality was never so clearly drawn. Her world blurred at the edges. What came to her in sleep often refused to fade with the morning light. Instead, it followed her — not like memory, but like *evidence*. And in sketching those visions, she did something radical: she treated dreams not as fantasy, but as *facts*.

This blurring — this constant teetering on the threshold between the imagined and the imminent — is perhaps the most fascinating and unsettling part of her legacy. Because when we ask whether her drawings were prophecies or coincidences, we're really circling a deeper question: *How much of what we call "reality" is already encoded in what we dream?*

For Ryo, the answer was instinctual. She didn't separate the two. She didn't wake up and say, "That wasn't real." Instead, she woke up and *drew*. Her act of creation was her act of acknowledgment. The dreams were treated with the same care, precision, and respect as a memory or a photograph. If it came in sleep, it was worth capturing. Not to prove anything. Not to convince anyone. But because the feeling of it — the emotional charge — lingered like truth.

And this is where most people begin to lose their footing. Because the more you engage with Ryo's drawings — their quietness, their eerie stillness, their emotional familiarity — the more you begin to wonder: *Have I seen this?* Not in real life, maybe. But in your *own* dreams. In a flash of déjà vu. In a recurring feeling you couldn't explain. That's what makes her work feel not just prophetic, but *recognizable*. It doesn't predict the future. It describes the inner terrain of a future-conscious mind.

Many spiritual traditions, especially in Japan, don't see a hard boundary between dreams and reality. In Shinto, the dream realm is considered one of many overlapping worlds. In Buddhism, dreams are vehicles for karmic information, reminders that the material world itself is a kind of illusion. Even in Western mysticism, the dream is seen as a bridge — a liminal state where the subconscious and superconscious briefly meet.

Ryo operated from this space intuitively. She didn't explain the mechanics. She didn't try to interpret her own work. She left that space open. And that openness is what gives her drawings power. If she had declared, "This is going to happen," they might have lost their magic. But she didn't. She simply asked, through her pencil and her silence: *What if it already has?*

One of her most haunting pieces is a drawing of a street where the shadows are longer than they should be. Everything looks normal — but the light feels wrong. The angle is off. The air is too still. There's no disaster, no action, just a *sensation*. And that's how dreams often speak — not in facts, but in *moods*. In atmospheres that cling to you long after you've woken.

In this way, Ryo's work teaches us that the line between dream and reality isn't a wall — it's a *membrane*. Porous. Shifting. It's where ideas pass through before they manifest. Where the subconscious whispers what the conscious mind hasn't yet learned how to say. And if you're sensitive — if you're open — you can feel those whispers. You can trace their outlines. Ryo did. And she sketched them not as fantasies, but as quiet maps of potential.

Some neuroscientists argue that dreams are the brain's way of processing and predicting — pattern recognition systems that simulate scenarios before they occur. If that's true, then maybe Ryo was just particularly attuned to that simulation.

Maybe she was picking up on the collective rhythms of an anxious planet. Or maybe, as some believe, she was simply one of those rare individuals who remembered *too clearly* what she saw on the other side of sleep.

This is the tension we live with, especially now, when the world often feels like it's catching up to some dream we've all had. Cities emptying. Skies thick with strange weather. Oceans rising. Clocks that no longer reassure us. It's not just about what's *happening* — it's about what's *been felt* for years. And Ryo's sketches, drawn long before those feelings turned into headlines, remind us that the future often arrives first through the unconscious.

So where is the line between dream and reality?

Maybe there isn't one.

Maybe the dream is just reality *remembered early*.

And maybe the only real difference between a prophet and a dreamer... is whether or not they're brave enough to draw what they see.

Ryo was.

And in doing so, she didn't just blur the line.

She taught us to *walk it*.

The Evolution of Her Predictions

Ryo Tatsuki never set out to become a prophet. She didn't declare a grand vision or create a timeline of global catastrophe. Her earliest dreams, recorded in the 1980s and early 1990s, were small, symbolic, and deeply personal. They hinted at emotions rather than events, and sketched quiet moments that felt more like psychological impressions than forecasts. And yet, as the decades passed, something undeniable began to take shape — a narrative arc within her dreams, a gradual sharpening of images, a subtle acceleration of intensity. Her predictions didn't just multiply. They *evolved*.

In the beginning, Ryo's dreams focused on ordinary places with slightly wrong atmospheres — a street where the shadows moved backward, a train station without people, a child staring up at a sky that looked "too new." These weren't predictions in the conventional sense. They were *moods*. A feeling of subtle distortion in familiar settings. She captured these feelings with haunting precision: muted tones, minimal text, vacant space. They weren't warnings. They were questions. And most readers at the time interpreted them as metaphor.

But in the mid-1990s, something changed. The first notable shift came with her vision of the Great Hanshin Earthquake — the Kobe disaster — which struck in January 1995. Thirteen years earlier, she had sketched collapsed buildings and named a date dangerously close to the actual event. This was the moment when her work started to be viewed through a prophetic lens. And it marked a change in *tone*. Her drawings became more detailed. Her captions more urgent. The dreams themselves — still soft and understated — now hinted at *consequence*.

From there, her predictions took on larger forms. The dreams became more specific, not just in geography, but in global mood. Cities flooded. Clocks stopped. Mountains cracked open. Her work in the late 1990s and early 2000s suggested a slow build toward something heavier, though never chaotic. Even in disaster, her art was calm. Still. As if she saw not the explosion, but the silence that followed it.

By the time she drew the masked people in public spaces — years before the COVID-19 pandemic — her dreams had begun to reflect a planet in emotional decline. Not just disasters, but *disconnection*. Not just physical events, but the *internal* consequences. One vision showed people standing next to each other without speaking, their shadows falling in opposite directions. Another depicted a hospital corridor where no one moved — not because they were dead, but because they had *stopped waiting*.

The evolution of Ryo's predictions wasn't just about scale — it was about *tone*. Early on, her sketches felt like echoes from a parallel world. Over time, they began to feel like echoes of *our* world — just slightly ahead of where we were standing. She moved from dreamlike impressions to emotionally grounded forecasts. It's as if her dreaming self had become more attuned, more honed, more precise. And the world, perhaps, was catching up to what she had been sensing all along.

Her most famous prediction — the vision tied to July 5, 2025, at 4:18 AM — is the culmination of this evolution. Not because it is the loudest or the most dramatic, but because it contains *everything* her previous dreams had hinted at: time, water, stillness, absence, and a figure watching from above. It doesn't scream. It doesn't explain. But it *knows*. It carries with it the full arc of her evolution — from dreamy impressions to collective premonition.

It's also worth noting how her *style* evolved alongside her content. Her early sketches were fluid, sometimes abstract, with little framing or structure. As her dreams became more intense, her lines became more controlled. Her use of white space more deliberate. Her figures more solitary. And in the last decade of her drawing, she began using *less*. Fewer details. Fewer words. As if clarity came not from adding, but from *removing* — stripping the dream to its most essential form.

What does this tell us?

It tells us that Ryo's journey as a visionary was not static. It grew with her. It deepened. It changed shape. Her dreams evolved as the world did. Or perhaps the world evolved to meet her dreams. Either way, there was a convergence — a slow tightening of the thread between the seen and the unseen.

For those who study her work today, this evolution provides a kind of roadmap. Not one that predicts exact events, but one that reveals *patterns*. A rising emotional temperature. A spiritual thinning of the boundary between what is and what is becoming. Her dreams weren't just about *what* might happen. They were about *how we are feeling* as we approach it.

In that way, the evolution of her predictions mirrors the evolution of the planet itself.

Quiet at first.

Then trembling.

Then waiting.

The Global Implications of Her Visions

When Ryo Tatsuki quietly began sketching the dreams she couldn't forget, she likely never imagined they would one day ripple across continents, cultures, and consciousness. What began as a personal record of mysterious inner visions became something far larger — a global conversation. And now, as more people discover her work, particularly in the shadow of the coming July 5, 2025 prediction, the implications of her drawings are being considered not just as individual symbols, but as *planetary reflections*. Because if even a portion of what she saw holds meaning beyond metaphor, then her work doesn't just matter to Japan — it matters to *everyone*.

Ryo never addressed global politics. Her drawings never named world leaders or economic systems. Yet embedded in her work is a quiet suggestion: that what we think of as national or local events are really *shared human experiences*. Earthquakes don't respect borders. Pandemics don't ask for passports. Water, fire, silence — these forces move through us all. And that is one of the deepest global implications of her visions: they dissolve the illusion of separation.

One of her most haunting images — a rising sea submerging a major port city — has been compared to cities from Yokohama to Jakarta to Rotterdam. The drawing contains no name, no language, just structures, shadows, and water. And that's the point. Her visions aren't geographically exclusive. They're emotionally global. They show what it *feels like* to face collapse, not just where it might happen. In doing so, her art speaks across language barriers and belief systems. It taps into something primal, collective, and unshakably human.

This universality is why her work has taken root in dream forums in Brazil, psychology circles in France, disaster-preparedness communities in Indonesia, and even spiritual groups in Nigeria. Each audience sees something of their own reality — or their own fear — reflected back. And more importantly, many feel something else too: *recognition*. As if her drawings are not predicting something new, but *revealing what we already sense deep inside*.

There is a quiet consensus forming among her global followers — one that transcends belief in prophecy or debate about accuracy. It's the idea that Ryo's visions serve as an emotional map of what it means to live in a world on the edge of transformation. Not just a physical one, but a psychological, spiritual, and social upheaval that affects everyone. Her drawings act as pressure readings from the soul of the species. And those readings are becoming harder to ignore.

One particularly striking implication lies in how her work reframes the concept of global disaster. Most media narratives portray collapse as sudden, explosive, filled with noise. But Ryo's world-ending dreams are quiet. Slow. Still. Her most famous timestamp — *4:18 AM* — suggests a moment not of eruption, but of *unseen transition*. Something happening while the world sleeps. Something we might miss — not because it's small, but because we've stopped listening.

That's what gives her visions such resonance on the world stage. In an age of technological overexposure and emotional desensitization, her drawings remind us that the most important changes may not be televised or tweeted. They may arrive like a dream you wake from in sweat, heart pounding, not knowing why. They may come with the smell of salt in the air, or the eerie sense that a clock has stopped ticking.

This emotional preparation — not logistical, but *intuitive* — is perhaps the most overlooked implication of her work. Governments prepare with drills. Scientists measure risk. But Ryo's drawings suggest we must also prepare our hearts, our awareness, our capacity to *be present in the unthinkable*. What if her drawings aren't warning us what to *prevent*, but showing us how to *stand in it* when it comes?

This leads to another implication: the question of *timing*. Her visions stretch across decades. Some seem to have come to pass already. Others, like the July 2025 dream, hover on the horizon like a wave not yet crested. But for many who've studied her work, time itself feels less like a sequence and more like a spiral — her dreams are less linear forecasts than pressure points on a larger cycle of awakening. If that's true, then her work isn't about predicting isolated disasters, but charting the emotional evolution of humanity itself.

In this light, Ryo's global role becomes clear: she's not a prophet in the conventional sense. She's more like an emotional cartographer — mapping not the world as it *is*, but as it *feels underneath*. And those maps, strangely, seem to align with where the world is going.

In a time of global climate anxiety, economic fragility, technological acceleration, and spiritual disorientation, her work gives people something rare: *stillness with meaning*. A moment to pause. To reflect. To ask: *What have we forgotten? What are we not seeing?* And more than anything: *What part of us already knows?*

Because maybe the biggest global implication of her visions isn't disaster.

Maybe it's *awakening*.

A collective remembrance of our intuition.

A re-sensitizing of the human heart.

A moment — not of collapse — but of convergence.

Of dreams and reality.

Of the past and the not-yet.

Of you, and me, and a woman who quietly drew what the rest of us were too distracted to see.

The Continuation of Her Work

Ryo Tatsuki never declared a legacy. She never claimed a mission. She simply dreamed, and then she drew. And when those drawings began to echo into the world with uncanny accuracy, she didn't step forward to lead a movement or define a philosophy. She remained still, quiet, and mysterious — just like her work. But now, long after many of her early visions have either materialized or rippled through public consciousness, the question becomes clear: *Who will continue what she started?*

The continuation of Ryo Tatsuki's work doesn't begin with imitation. No one can—or should—try to replicate her dreams. Her gift wasn't a technique. It wasn't a style. It was a state of being. A willingness to *listen* to what came through her. Her legacy, then, is not a body of images to be copied, but a *practice* of seeing, receiving, and recording the unseen with honesty and humility.

In the years since her work resurfaced globally, a quiet but growing circle of artists, writers, and intuitives have begun following a similar path. They're not all visionaries. Some are dream diarists, quietly sketching fragments from their sleep. Others are filmmakers creating atmospheres inspired by premonition. Poets writing from dreams that feel more like memories. Psychologists and spiritual teachers encouraging the use of dreams not just as inner guidance, but as *collective sensing tools*. These are not disciples. They are *responders* — people who have felt the ripple of Ryo's work and now move with it.

The continuation of her work can also be seen in the evolving relationship between creativity and intuition. Her influence is now embedded in how a generation of artists treat the mysterious: with care, with space, with reverence. Her restraint has taught others to *feel deeply without forcing meaning*. Her drawings whisper: *You don't have to know what it means to honor what you saw.*

And while Ryo never left a formal method, many have organically adopted her process: waking early, drawing immediately, noting time and mood, capturing the vision before the conscious mind scrambles it. This simple ritual — *wake, remember, draw* — has become a sacred act for those who feel connected to her energy. It's not about prophecy. It's about *preservation*. Holding on to what might otherwise vanish.

In Japan, a number of small dream-artist collectives have formed, sharing monthly sketches and symbolic entries, not for profit or praise, but to participate in what they call *emotional mapping*. They cite Ryo not as a prophet, but as a pioneer of spiritual cartography — someone who dared to draw the intangible, and in doing so, reminded the rest of us that inner worlds matter.

Internationally, her work has influenced not just artists, but *designers of awareness*. Architects thinking about stillness in public spaces. Therapists using dream recall to guide emotional healing. Even AI researchers are studying her art to understand how humans process uncertainty and intuition — how we turn glimpses of possibility into shape, texture, and symbol.

What's most fascinating, however, is that the continuation of her work doesn't belong to a single medium. It's not just in dream-art or premonitory sketches. It's in the way people are starting to *honor subtlety*. The quiet nudge. The inner knowing. The image that appears before understanding arrives. Ryo didn't just show us how to draw the future — she showed us how to *trust the present moment when it feels like something's shifting*.

Perhaps that's the ultimate continuation of her work — the revival of *trust in inner knowing*. Her legacy lives in everyone who pauses when they feel a strange silence. In those who write down a dream because it felt too real. In those who sketch something they can't explain. In those who stare out the window at 4:18 AM and wonder, *Why do I feel this right now?*

Some say that others will rise with similar gifts — dreamers who will begin to draw what's coming. Not because they seek fame, but because the visions will demand to be seen. Maybe those dreamers are already here, quietly working in sketchbooks, waking with the feeling that something wants to come through them. And maybe they, like Ryo, will not explain themselves.

They will simply *draw*.

And in that act — that sacred, simple act — Ryo Tatsuki's work will continue. Not in repetition, but in *resonance*. Not as a prophecy line, but as a pulse moving through time.

Because her drawings were never the end of something.

They were the beginning.

The invitation to listen deeper.

And to draw what waits in the dark... before the world gives it a name.

The Public's Role in Heeding Warnings

Prophets do not shape the future alone. Artists and visionaries like Ryo Tatsuki may receive the dream, may draw the symbols, may offer the glimpses — but the weight of what happens next never rests on their shoulders alone. The burden, ultimately, belongs to *us*. To the public. Because what we choose to do — or not do — with a warning is what determines whether it becomes a tragedy, a lesson, or a turning point. And that places the public not as passive viewers of Ryo's work, but as *participants* in the prophecy.

For years, Ryo's drawings circulated quietly. The early zines, passed from hand to hand, reached a small, almost secretive community. But as events in the real world began to mirror her work, particularly after the 2011 tsunami and the spread of the COVID-19 pandemic, something shifted. The public took notice. They began to *look back* at what she had seen years before — the waves, the silence, the masks, the dates. And what they found wasn't a perfectly outlined forecast. What they found was *recognition*.

But recognition is not the same as response.

To heed a warning requires more than belief. It requires engagement. Discernment. Sometimes even action. And that's where things get complicated. Because Ryo's drawings don't tell people what to do. They don't give directions. They're not loud, they're not dramatic, and they're certainly not instructive. They require *interpretation*. And the public's role is to step into that ambiguity and decide, collectively and individually, what it *means*.

That process, for many, begins with intuition — the personal sense that *this drawing is speaking to me*. The feeling that something in it aligns with a private anxiety, a recurring dream, a silent knowing. But what happens next? Do we forget? Do we share it? Do we prepare? Or do we wait until the moment passes — and only then look back in hindsight?

In some ways, the modern world is trained to ignore quiet warnings. We're conditioned to act only when headlines shout. And that's part of the challenge with Ryo's work. Her warnings don't arrive as breaking news. They arrive in pencil. In metaphor. In mood. And it's up to the public to cultivate the kind of awareness required to *hear* that.

Some have. All over the world, individuals and small communities have begun treating her work not as prediction, but as *prompt*. They've used it to reflect, to discuss, to prepare emotionally. In Japan, families living near the coast have quietly revisited their emergency plans after encountering her sketches. Dreamers across cultures have started to record their own visions more carefully, inspired by Ryo's integrity and patience. And in quiet spaces online, people are asking deeper questions — not just about the dreams, but about their *own response* to them.

But public response also risks distortion. Some turn her images into spectacle. Some sensationalize, commercialize, dramatize what was never meant to be loud. This is a critical challenge: when a warning becomes a trend, it loses its stillness. And without stillness, we can't hear what the dream is saying.

To truly heed a warning means to sit with it. To not rush into conclusions. To not weaponize it, or dismiss it, but to *live with the question it raises*. Ryo's dreams don't ask for panic. They ask for *presence*. They ask the public to feel, to reflect, to consider their surroundings — not just geographically, but spiritually. Are we paying attention? Are we treating the earth like something sacred? Are we listening to each other? Are we listening to ourselves?

This is the deeper role of the public in responding to prophecy: *inner preparation*. Not just moving to higher ground or storing food — but becoming *emotionally aware* of where we are in the arc of things. The drawing of the rooftop man doesn't just ask, "What will you do when the water comes?" It asks, "Who will you be when it does?"

Because that's what prophecy is for.

Not control.

Not fear.

But *readiness*.

And Ryo's work, in its quiet grace, asks something radical of the public: to be more than witnesses. To become *interpreters. Translators. Responders.* Not in the sense of proving the visions true or false, but in choosing to grow because of them. Choosing to shift. Choosing to trust what you feel in the moment when the world goes quiet.

Ultimately, it is not enough for prophets to dream. The dreams must be *received*.

And that is where the future — our future — begins.

The Final Chapter: Awaiting July 2025

For years now, Ryo Tatsuki's name has been softly echoed in circles of curiosity and reverence. Not by her own doing, but because her quiet pencil lines, once confined to obscure dream journals, began to resemble the world as it would become. And among all the fragments she left behind — the rising seas, the masked figures, the unnatural silence — one moment stands out. A date. A time. A feeling that continues to ripple through hearts and conversations alike:

July 5, 2025 — 4:18 AM.

This is the dream that many return to, again and again. Not because it is the most detailed or dramatic, but because of its stillness. In the sketch, there is no explosion. No fire or scream. Just a flooded landscape, a sky that seems too pale, a rooftop figure watching the water like he's been waiting his whole life to see it arrive. It's this moment — poised between event and observation — that has captivated thousands. And now, with that date approaching fast, the world finds itself not in chaos, but in a kind of *collective pause*.

What does it mean to wait for a prophecy?

This is the strange emotional terrain so many find themselves navigating — not knowing what to expect, but knowing they *expect something*. Some see July 2025 as a fixed point, something inevitable. Others believe it may pass quietly, as many dates do, without a single headline. Still others believe the true significance of the moment will not be external, but internal — an awakening, a shift, a deepening of some kind. Something that won't be measured by earthquakes or tsunamis, but by how it *feels* to be human on that morning.

There are people who will stay up all night. People who will meditate at dawn. People who will gather online, watching the hour pass as if it's a celestial alignment. And there are also people who will forget — or who will wake that morning, sip coffee, and not realize until much later what day it was.

But perhaps that, too, is part of the mystery.

Because Ryo never told us *what* would happen. She didn't describe a precise disaster. She didn't scream for action. She simply wrote the time, and drew the moment. That restraint has allowed the dream to become something more than a prediction. It has become a *mirror*. People look into it and see their own concerns reflected. Environmental anxieties. Political unrest. The fragile sense that the world is shifting — slowly, silently, and possibly forever.

What awaits us in July 2025 is not just a date. It's a *threshold*. A point that has collected enough meaning, speculation, and emotion to become something sacred, even if nothing physical occurs. And in that sense, it might be the most Ryo-like moment of all — quiet, symbolic, incomplete. A page left open.

Many of Ryo's followers describe feeling like they're "approaching something," but they can't name what. It's less about fear, and more about *readiness*. A kind of emotional posture. Like standing at the edge of a long hallway, hearing something move in the distance, but not yet knowing whether it's a whisper, a wave, or your own heartbeat.

And maybe that's the gift of her final dream.

It brings us back to *attention*.

To the sky.

To the ground.

To the water.

To the clocks on our walls.

To the feeling that *time is not only passing — it is becoming*.

As July approaches, some are preparing. Some are watching. Some are letting go.

But all of us — in some way, large or small — are participating.

And in doing so, we honor what Ryo Tatsuki gave us:

Not fear.

Not control.

But presence.

So whether the world changes on that morning or not, whether the sea rises or the wind shifts or nothing happens at all, we will have *felt* something together.

We will have remembered to *look*.

And in that, maybe, the dream has already come true.

I hope you found wisdom within these pages. If you liked this book, please leave a review where you bought it. Thank you from the author.

About the Author

Andrew Parry is a dedicated researcher and writer with a deep fascination for the paranormal, the unknown, and the metaphysical. His work delves into the mysteries that lie beyond the limits of conventional understanding, exploring everything from ghostly encounters and unexplained phenomena to theories of consciousness, time, and alternate dimensions.

Read more at https://lonetrail.blog.

www.ingramcontent.com/pod-product-compliance
Lightning Source LLC
Chambersburg PA
CBHW060314300425
25945CB00014BA/1069